A USER'S GUIDE TO MELANCHOLY

A User's Guide to Melancholy takes Robert Burton's encyclopaedic masterpiece *The Anatomy of Melancholy* (first published in 1621) as a guide to one of the most perplexing, elusive, attractive, and afflicting diseases of the Renaissance. Burton's *Anatomy* is perhaps the largest, strangest, and most unwieldy self-help book ever written. Engaging with the rich cultural and literary framework of melancholy, this book traces its causes, symptoms, and cures through Burton's writing. Each chapter starts with a case study of melancholy – from the man who was afraid to urinate in case he drowned his town to the girl who purged a live eel – as a way into exploring the many facets of this mental affliction. *A User's Guide to Melancholy* presents in an accessible and illustrated format the colourful variety of Renaissance melancholy, and contributes to contemporary discussions about well-being by revealing the earlier history of mental health conditions.

MARY ANN LUND is Associate Professor in Renaissance English Literature at the University of Leicester. She is the author of *Melancholy, Medicine and Religion in Early Modern England: Reading 'The Anatomy of Melancholy'* (Cambridge University Press, 2010) which was shortlisted for The Council for College and University English Book Prize. She has contributed to the BBC Radio 4 series *In Our Time* on *The Anatomy of Melancholy* (2011), *The Glass Delusion* (2015), and *A History of Delusions* (2018). She was an Arts and Humanities Research Council Leadership Fellow (2015–17) and edited *The Oxford Edition of the Sermons of John Donne: Vol. 12* (2018).

A USER'S GUIDE TO MELANCHOLY

MARY ANN LUND
University of Leicester

CAMBRIDGE
UNIVERSITY PRESS

CAMBRIDGE
UNIVERSITY PRESS

University Printing House, Cambridge CB2 8BS, United Kingdom

One Liberty Plaza, 20th Floor, New York, NY 10006, USA

477 Williamstown Road, Port Melbourne, VIC 3207, Australia

314–321, 3rd Floor, Plot 3, Splendor Forum, Jasola District Centre, New Delhi – 110025, India

79 Anson Road, #06–04/06, Singapore 079906

Cambridge University Press is part of the University of Cambridge.

It furthers the University's mission by disseminating knowledge in the pursuit of education, learning, and research at the highest international levels of excellence.

www.cambridge.org
Information on this title: www.cambridge.org/9781108838849
DOI: 10.1017/9781108978996

First published 2021

Printed in the United Kingdom by TJ Books Limited, Padstow Cornwall

A catalogue record for this publication is available from the British Library.

Library of Congress Cataloging-in-Publication Data
NAMES: Lund, Mary Ann, 1978–author.
TITLE: A user's guide to melancholy / Mary Ann Lund.
DESCRIPTION: Cambridge ; New York, NY : Cambridge University Press, 2021. | Includes bibliographical references and index.
IDENTIFIERS: LCCN 2020050617 | ISBN 9781108838849 (hardback) | ISBN 9781108972444 (paperback) | ISBN 9781108978996 (ebook)
SUBJECTS: MESH: Burton, Robert, 1577–1640. Anatomy of melancholy. | Depressive Disorder | Depression | Medicine in Literature | History, Medieval
CLASSIFICATION: LCC RC537 | NLM WM 171.5 | DDC 616.85/27–dc23
LC record available at https://lccn.loc.gov/2020050617

ISBN 978-1-108-83884-9 Hardback

For Joseph and Hannah

CONTENTS

FIGURES

ACKNOWLEDGEMENTS

I would like to thank Emily Hockley at Cambridge University Press for encouraging me to write this book and for being a warm and supportive editor; Rachel Blaifeder, Emma Goff-Leggett, Bethany Johnson, Aloysias Saint Thomas and their teams for their hard work to bring this book to life; Damian Love for his excellent copy-editing; Bethlem Museum of the Mind and the UK Defence Academy in Shrivenham for inviting me to speak about melancholy, and the audiences for enthusiastic and stimulating discussions afterwards; James Yarker and Stan's Cafe for performing the *Anatomy* and helping me to think about it in new ways; Victoria Shepherd for inspiring radio programmes about delusions; my colleagues and students at the University of Leicester; friends and neighbours; my family, especially my parents, Clare and John; and most of all, Gareth, Joseph, and Hannah, with love and gratitude for mirth and merry company.

ABBREVIATIONS AND NOTE ON THE TEXT

Unless otherwise stated, all quotations from the *Anatomy* are taken from Robert Burton, *The Anatomy of Melancholy*, ed. Holbrook Jackson (New York Review Books, 2001). This one-volume edition starts the page numbering again with each 'Partition', of which there are three (the first one also includes Burton's long preface, 'Democritus Junior to the Reader'). My references take the form of the Partition number in roman numerals followed by the page number, e.g. 'ii.200' is Partition 2, p. 200. I use the abbreviation 'Burton, *Anatomy*' where necessary.

Burton conventionally uses Latinised names when referring to his sources, e.g. 'Montanus'. I refer to them by their vernacular names, e.g. 'Giambattista da Monte', and give the Latin name (if it is significantly different) and, where known, dates in parentheses. These details are taken from the 'Biobibliographical Index' found in vol. VI of *The Anatomy of Melancholy*, ed. Thomas C. Faulkner, Nicolas K. Kiessling, and Rhonda L. Blair; commentary by J. B. Bamborough with Martin Dodsworth, 6 vols. (Oxford: Clarendon Press, 1989–2000). This edition is referred to throughout as *Anatomy*, ed. Faulkner *et al.*

Bible quotations are taken from the King James Version (unless otherwise stated) and are taken from *The Bible in English Database* (Chadwick-Healey, 1996).

I have modernised the spelling and lightly modernised punctuation of all quotations from Renaissance texts.

Introduction

> They will act, conceive all extremes, contrarieties, and contradictions, and that in infinite varieties … Scarce two of two thousand that concur in the same symptoms. The tower of Babel never yielded such confusion of tongues, as the chaos of melancholy doth variety of symptoms. There is in all melancholy *similitudo dissimilis*, like men's faces, a disagreeing likeness still; and as in a river we swim in the same place, though not in the same numerical water; as the same instrument affords several lessons, so the same disease yields diversity of symptoms.
>
> (Burton, *Anatomy*, i.397)

In recent years, the question of how varieties of mental distress should be categorised has been the subject of significant debate. Should a wide range of conditions such as bipolar disorder, schizophrenia, and major depression be treated as discrete disorders? One of the major authorities on the subject, the American Psychiatric Association's *Diagnostic and Statistical Manual of Mental Disorders*, does exactly that. Or should they be recognised instead as overlapping conditions, with mental health problems being seen as existing on a spectrum with 'normal' experience? The boundaries between different formal categories can be paper-thin, and many people who suffer from mental distress have a mixture of complaints and symptoms. The British Psychological Society has suggested that a better approach than applying different diagnostic labels would be to work 'from the bottom up', paying attention to individuals' specific experiences, problems, and symptoms.[1]

Medical writers in sixteenth- and seventeenth-century Europe might have recognised some of the issues at stake in this debate, since they frequently acknowledged how diverse and varied problems of the mind could be. As Robert Burton, author of *The Anatomy of Melancholy*, puts it, there is a 'disagreeing likeness' between them. Yet he and his contemporaries would have had far fewer difficulties with what to call them, since they used one name above all to describe a very wide spectrum of experience: melancholy. Renaissance melancholy certainly includes the kind of sadness and mournful pensiveness we might mean when we use the word today. But it also encompasses delusions, anxiety, griefs, phobias, and a whole range of allied physical symptoms such as trapped wind, migraines, and skin rashes. Melancholics might be spotted by their outward behaviour: their tendency to seek out solitude and to sit lost in their own thoughts and fantasies, or to act in bizarre ways (say, laughing for hours at a single joke, or believing that they are made of glass). Then again, they may appear entirely normal but, like Hamlet, have 'that within which passeth show'.[2]

The subject of this book is a condition of mental distress with ancient origins. The word 'melancholy' derives from the Greek for the humour black bile (*μελαν-* dark, + *χολή* bile), and it was discussed by the Father of Medicine, Hippocrates. Yet it reached its highest prominence during the sixteenth and seventeenth centuries, a period when melancholy came to be perceived as a European epidemic and when physicians and philosophers devoted many volumes to examining its causes, symptoms, and cures.[3] At the same time, it became a source of fascination to artists and literary writers, as a condition that both inspired creative genius and threatened to tip them into madness. The pseudo-Aristotelian *Problems* had posed the question: 'Why is it that all those men who have become extraordinary in philosophy, politics, poetry or the arts are obviously melancholic, and some to such an extent that they are seized by the illnesses that come from black bile?' That association between melancholy, creativity, and intellectual prowess, expanded upon by Marsilio Ficino in his *De Vita* (1498), cast a dark glamour over the condition which appealed to self-fashioning young aristocrats of the sixteenth century.[4]

The common definition of melancholy in the sixteenth and seventeenth centuries is as 'a kind of dotage without a fever, having for his ordinary companions fear, and sadness, without any apparent occasion' (i.169–70). But in the lived experience of individual sufferers, the disease easily escapes the bounds of this definition. Men, women, and even children were diagnosed with the condition, and although it was more commonly found among the rich – as might be expected, since they could afford to pay for the services of physicians – it was not exclusive to one class, race, sex, or profession. One of Burton's sources tells of a baker in the Italian city of Ferrara who succumbed to melancholy and became convinced that he was made of butter, to the extent that he dared not go near his oven or sit in the sun in case he melted. Monarchs fell prey to the disease, among them King Charles VI and King Louis XI of France. Melancholy might lead a sufferer towards irretrievable despair; then again, it might make him believe he was a shellfish.

A User's Guide to Melancholy explores this most slippery of conditions through the stories of individuals who suffered from it, and through the structures by which Renaissance medicine understood its causes, symptoms, and cures. To be a melancholic is to be subject to a Protean disorder, characterised as much by its 'infinite varieties' as by what two cases might have in common. It is dangerous, perhaps even leading the patient towards suicide. Yet it is Siren-like and alluring, promising the pleasurable life of solitude, leisure, and contemplation before it traps its victim into an inescapable cycle of loneliness and self-destructive thought patterns.

Through an examination of Renaissance melancholy, this book also explores Robert Burton's encyclopaedic masterpiece *The Anatomy of Melancholy*, first published four hundred years ago in 1621 and perhaps the largest, strangest, and most unwieldy self-help book ever written (Figure 0.1). It is *A User's Guide* both because it aims to navigate the complexities and quirks of Burton's book, and because the *Anatomy* is itself designed to be used by – and to help – those who suffer from melancholy. Burton was an Oxford academic and his book is interested in documenting the attitudes and responses to melancholic disorder taken by physicians, philosophers, theologians, and poets over two millennia from ancient Greece to seventeenth-century Europe. But his approach is also distinctly practical, tracing the contours of the disease for the benefit of people afflicted by it, and including therapeutic measures that his readers can put into practice. One of the therapies is the act of reading itself: an activity that diverts, occupies, and consoles a grieving mind.

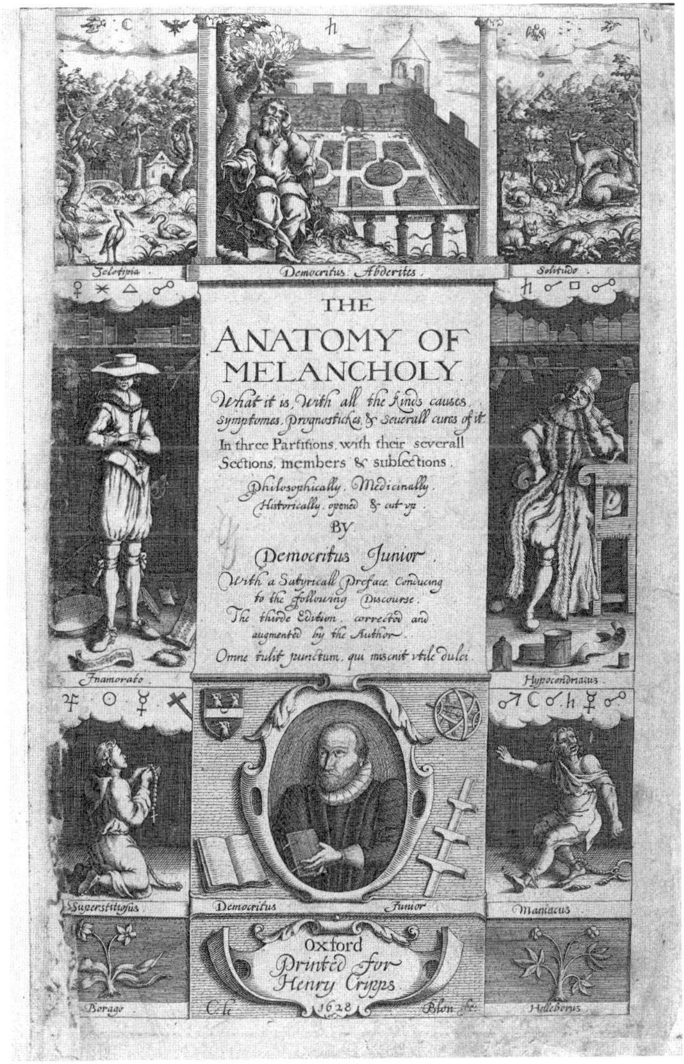

FIGURE 0.1 Frontispiece to *The Anatomy of Melancholy* (1628).

Democritus Junior, Robert Burton

When Robert Burton published *The Anatomy of Melancholy*, he did so, not under his own name, but under the guise of 'Democritus Junior'. In his opening words to the reader, he makes much of his pseudonym, imagining that the reader will be curious to know who he really is:

> Gentle reader, I presume thou wilt be very inquisitive to know what antic or personate actor this is, that so insolently intrudes upon this common theatre, to the world's view, arrogating another man's name; whence he is, why he doth it, and what he hath to say; although, as he said, *Primum si noluero, non respondebo, quis coacturus est?* I am a free man born, and may choose whether I will tell; who can compel me? if I be urged, I will as readily reply as that Egyptian in Plutarch, when a curious fellow would needs know what he had in his basket, *Quum vides velatam, quid inquiris in rem absconditam?* It was therefore covered, because he should not know what was in it. Seek not after that which is hid; if the contents please thee, "and be for thy use, suppose the Man in the Moon, or whom thou wilt to be the author"; I would not willingly be known. (i.16)

The extract shows us several important aspects of the way Burton writes. The first thing we might notice is that he speaks to the reader directly – an unexpected technique to find in a medical textbook, at least by our modern standards. Though Burton sounds scholarly, his language is also conversational; we can imagine him saying these words like a character speaking a monologue on stage. He himself, of course, introduces the idea that he is a performer in 'this common theatre', the world. Though his subject is melancholy, Burton is so interested in his reader that he tells us, 'thou thyself art the subject of my discourse' (i.16). This is more than simply a manual about a disease; or rather, it is about a disease that also encompasses the many facets of human experience. Though habitual melancholy – the kind that sticks – is a chronic condition that has causes, symptoms, and cures, in a broader sense, melancholy is something that afflicts us all: it is 'the character of mortality' (i.144).

Another thing we might notice in this extract is how often Burton intersperses his own words with those of other people, often in Latin (though he tends to follow them up with a translation). While this was a common technique in writing of the time, even so, Burton quotes more than most of his contemporaries. The biographer Anthony Wood notes that he was famous for this habit: 'no man in his time did surpass him for his ready and dexterous interlarding his common discourses among them with verses from the poets, or sentences from classic authors'.[5] Not only using another man's name, he also uses other men's words. As he declares – typically using a quotation from someone else – 'I have only this of Macrobius to say for myself, *Omne meum, nihil meum*, 'tis all mine, and none mine' (i.24).

And, as the passage shows all too well, Burton is a playful, elusive writer. He is teasing and provocative, sometimes ingratiating ('Gentle reader'), then at the next moment defiant ('who can compel me?'). He writes about a slippery disease in a slippery way – and about a condition of sorrow with exuberance. He revels in paradox and contradiction, often gathering different authorities on melancholy who disagree, setting them against one another. Though his opening paragraph sounds like a monologue, his writing style also often sounds like dialogue – and, on occasion, a near-cacophanous debate of competing voices and opinions. What Burton's own opinion on a given point is, is not always easy to tell. The fact that he speaks from behind the persona of Democritus Junior makes the task even harder – and Burton deliberately frustrates our curiosity about who he is or what he thinks.

Why does the writer of *The Anatomy of Melancholy* choose to play the role of Democritus Junior? His name declares the author to be the heir of the ancient Greek philosopher. One early source tells the story of how the people of Abdera asked Hippocrates, the father of Western medicine, to visit Democritus because they were concerned that their local philosopher had gone mad. Hippocrates found him in his garden surrounded by the corpses of animals and asked him what he was doing. Democritus replied that he was dissecting them in order to search for the source of madness, since he had observed that folly afflicted the whole world. Hippocrates could only agree, and told the citizens of Abdera that Democritus was not mad at all, but rather was the wisest of men.

When Burton retells this anecdote, he has Democritus looking for the origins not only of madness, but of melancholy. In so doing, he broadens the spectrum of mental distress which was within the scope of Democritus' enquiry, and by extension his own. Following in his footsteps, Democritus Junior does the same task through the printed page, trying to prove along the way that 'all the world is mad, that it is melancholy' (i.39): hence why his book is anatomising melancholy.

There is a further reason for the pseudonym. Democritus was known as the laughing philosopher, who found the world's follies so absurd that he could only laugh at them, unlike his counterpart Heraclitus, whose response to the madness and misery of human lives was to weep (Figure 0.2). In Erasmus' *Praise of Folly* (1511), Folly herself tells her audience that these days there are so many new forms of madness that 'a thousand Democrituses wouldn't be enough to laugh at them, and we'd always have to call in one Democritus more'.[6] Following in Folly's footsteps, Burton becomes the newest Democritus of his age, satirically mocking the foolishness of the world.

FIGURE 0.2 *Democritus Laughs.* Anonymous, after Jan van der Bruggen (1661–1726).

This might seem a surprising aim for someone whose task is also to cure mental distress. But Burton sees the two as interlinked. The grief of mind suffered by individuals is a symptom of wider malaise: war and violence, religious superstition, corrupt magistrates and politicians, unjust laws, people motivated only by greed and ambition. 'Would this, think you', he says as he surveys the recent history of massacres and genocide, 'have enforced our Democritus to laughter, or rather made him turn his tune, alter his tone, and weep with Heraclitus?' (i.59). Anatomising melancholy is a moral and political project, one that demands a 'mixed passion' where he sometimes laughs, sometimes angrily rails, sometimes laments and sympathises with the human misery that breeds melancholy (i.19, 59).

And what of Robert Burton (1577–1640), the man behind the pseudonym? Burton tells his reader that, like Democritus, 'I have lived a silent, sedentary, solitary, private life … penned up most part in my study' (i.17). That study was in Oxford, where he spent all of his adult life.[7] He was born in rural Leicestershire, the younger son of a gentry family. After studying at the local grammar schools he went to Brasenose College, Oxford, but his undergraduate studies were interrupted for reasons unknown. His age matches the twenty-year-old Robert Burton who consulted the renowned astrological physician Simon Forman in 1597 with symptoms of melancholy, and whose history was recorded in Forman's case notes. Whether or not this was the same man, we cannot be sure. Nevertheless, the author of what is now called the *Anatomy* (it was known as 'Burton's *Melancholy*' in the seventeenth century) claimed to know the disease through personal experience.

Burton eventually completed his degree at Christ Church, Oxford, where he spent the rest of his life as a Student (or college Fellow). He probably worked on the *Anatomy* for more than a decade before it was first published in 1621. Not only did he search for source material – and therapy – in the Oxford libraries where he lived and worked, but he also built up his own collection of 1,700 books, eventually bequeathed to the Bodleian Library and Christ Church, and most of which can still be found there today. His handwritten notes bear the traces of his preoccupations as both a reader and a writer: words such as 'Causes', 'Symptoms', and 'Cures' are written in the margins of the medical textbooks he owned.[8]

Perhaps he was looking for self-treatment when he wrote these words, but he was also designing the structure of his book. He tells his reader that he has written it 'as a good housewife out of divers fleeces weaves one piece of cloth', finding source material in all of his reading. 'I have laboriously collected this cento out of divers authors', he says, a cento being both a patchwork and an ancient style of poetry made entirely out of quotations from other authors. One of the best known is a fourth-century poem in praise of Christ, composed from lines of Virgil by Faltonia Betitia Proba. Burton places himself in a tradition of writing with female associations: it is a humble, industrious task, in which 'the method only is mine own' (i.24–5), a far cry from the more ambitious claims to textual authority made by some of his contemporaries.

Despite his claims of staying confined to his study, biographical evidence shows that he lived a fairly active life. Like many academic scholars of his age he was also a clergyman. He was vicar of St Thomas', Oxford (a college living) from 1616 onwards, and from 1632 he was also rector of Seagrave in his home county of Leicestershire. The patron who presented him to this parish was George, eighth Baron Berkeley, who had studied at Christ Church and to whom Burton had dedicated *The Anatomy of Melancholy*. No doubt the living was a reward, but Burton appears to have treated his positions as more than simply income generators: he discharged his pastoral responsibilities at St Thomas' himself and, though he had a curate at Seagrave, he visited the parish in the summer months.

At Christ Church he was college librarian and he also held the post of clerk of Oxford market for several years. He wrote Latin drama that was performed in his college. The college's rules forbade him to marry, but a Latin poem prefacing the *Anatomy* proclaims the author's fondness for serving wenches, and he had a reputation for cheeriness. While he 'never travelled but in map or card, in which mine unconfined thoughts have freely expatiated' (i.18), he had a special interest in geography and surveying (his older brother William wrote a history of Leicestershire).

Describing himself in the *Anatomy*, he freely admits to having 'an unconstant, unsettled mind'. He expands on this with disarming self-deprecation:

> This roving humour … I have ever had, and like a ranging spaniel, that barks at every bird he sees, leaving his game, I have followed all, saving that which I should … I have read many books, but to little purpose, for want of good method; I have confusedly tumbled over divers authors in our libraries, with small profit for want of art, order, memory, judgment. (i.17–18).

His omnivorous interests are apparent in the *Anatomy*, the scope of which takes in not only medicine but moral philosophy, religion, ancient and modern history, geography, natural sciences, poetry, and even romantic love. Like Shakespeare's Autolycus, Burton was a snapper-up of unconsidered trifles. After the first edition appeared in 1621, he continued to add further examples, anecdotes, quotations, words, and phrases to his book over five further editions (the sixth came out in 1651, eleven years after his death); the book grew to over half a million words. Melancholy as the character of mortality is an endlessly varied, proliferating disease, and Burton's attempt to chart it is propelled by his curiosity – not always in a straight line.

Structure of this Book

There are two basic forms of medieval and Renaissance medical textbook, and the design of *A User's Guide to Melancholy* takes inspiration from them both. One is the form that Burton chose for the *Anatomy*: an examination of a disease from causes through to symptoms and cures (some, including Burton's, also included prognostics). This form provided a theoretical framework, drawn from the medical tradition established by the first-century Greek physician Galen, through which illness could be understood at a general level. Burton's own book is structured in a complex series of units and subunits – Partitions, Sections, Members, Subsections – as he moves from the general to the more specific, as can be seen from the branching diagrams published at the beginning of each Partition (Figure 0.3).

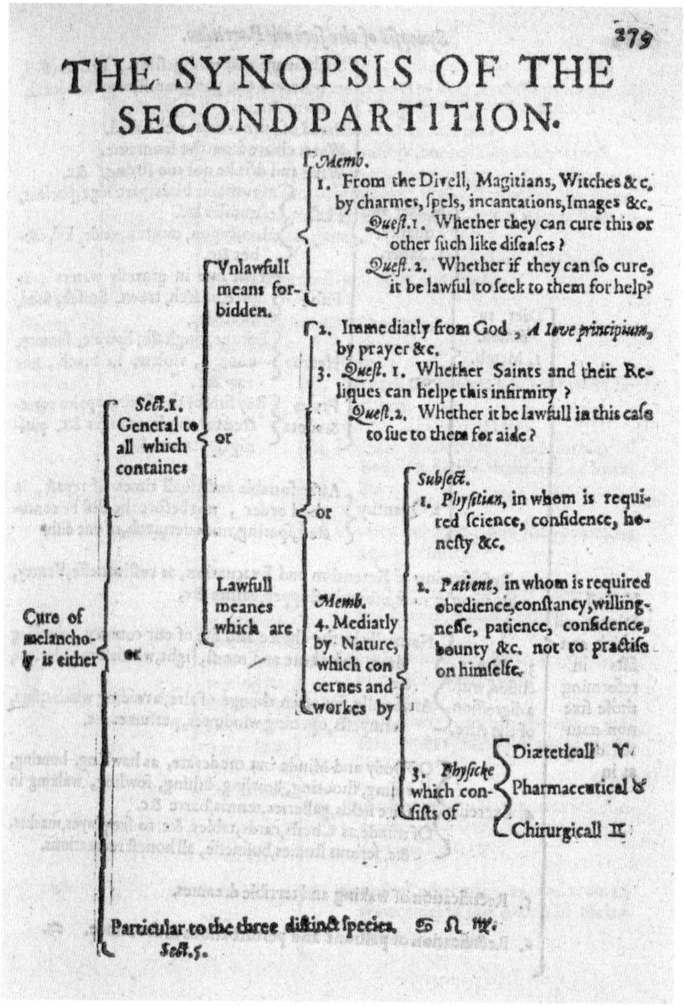

FIGURE 0.3 Synopsis of the Second Partition of *The Anatomy of Melancholy* (1621).

The other form of medical writing is the *consilium*: the collection of patient case histories compiled by an individual physician, along with the advice he gave and the treatments he prescribed. The *consilium* takes its lead from Hippocratic medicine, which held that the key to understanding a disease was to be found in the careful observation of individual cases. While a general study of a disease might establish broad rules and principles, in real patient bodies it might behave in wildly different ways and throw up a range of exceptions. As Burton remarks, 'the four-and-twenty letters make no more variety of words in divers languages than melancholy conceits produce diversity of symptoms in several persons' (i.408).

Intrinsic both to the *Anatomy* and to this book are the individual stories of melancholics. Each chapter of *A User's Guide* starts with a case study from the *Anatomy* or other Renaissance textbooks on melancholy: from an Italian man who was afraid of urinating to a Flemish girl who defecated an eel, from a Jewish Frenchman who died of fear *after* he had crossed a dangerous bridge to Burton himself, 'Democritus Junior', who claims that his expertise came from his own, intimate knowledge of 'melancholising'. These stories illuminate the rich variety of melancholic experience and also demonstrate how mental trouble was seen to be linked to various states and conditions of life: age and bodily temperament (including puberty), race, religious belief, gender, sexual appetite, profession, and personal habits.

Though *A User's Guide* is arranged from cause to cure, many facets of melancholy do not fit tidily into one category. For example, a bad fright may be a cause of melancholy but fear can also be a major symptom of the condition. Listening to music is excellent therapy for it, but in some cases it can exacerbate the condition or trigger it in the first place. Causes, symptoms, and cures bleed into one another, and what may be good for one person may be disastrous for another. The first two chapters discuss the major defining features of melancholy. It is a disease of the passions – sorrow and fear – and it is also a bodily experience, deriving from an excess or corruption of bodily humours. In Chapter 3, we consider the role of witchcraft, spirits, and otherworldly beings in melancholy. While Burton gives space to spiritual influences as a possible cause, he is also careful to insist that superstitious explanations can be attributed to phenomena which are simply physical in origin.

The symptoms of melancholy are the subject of the next three chapters. Chapter 4 centres on the wide variety of forms in which melancholic delusion manifested, while Chapter 5 addresses the special category of love or 'heroic' (erotic) melancholy and its relationship with gender and sexual activity. In Chapter 6, we look at the loss of hope – one of melancholy's most dangerous symptoms – through an extended attention to the story of Francis Spira, the man who died of despair after thinking he had been damned by God.

Physicians of Burton's time placed great emphasis on the role of the 'non-naturals' in the regulation of the self, and these introduce the subject of cures in Chapter 7: activities such as diet and exercise were seen to influence one's health and wellbeing. Chapter 8 considers the pharmaceutical and surgical remedies for melancholy: from herbal treatments such as hellebore to mineral talismans, bloodletting, and trepanning. In Chapter 9, we consider how Burton addresses healing for the perturbations of the mind through persuasion, consolation, distraction, and cheerfulness. Finally, we turn back to melancholy itself as a paradoxical condition, and look too at the *Anatomy*'s influence down the centuries.

A final note about words and names: wherever possible, this book tries to use words that Burton and his contemporaries in Renaissance England would have recognised when speaking about this disease. In the sixteenth and seventeenth centuries, people did not *have* melancholy; they *were* melancholic. To those who treated them, they were patients or sufferers rather than clients. They called the condition 'melancholy'; the word 'melancholia' was only very rarely used, and usually then only in medical texts with reference to the Latin. Melancholia now carries a sense of 'gloominess, a theatrical or aesthetic indulgence in reflective or maudlin emotion' (as the *OED* describes it) which is alien to the way Robert Burton would have understood melancholy, and which is outside the scope of this book.[9]

The word 'psychology' was first used in English in 1654, fourteen years after Robert Burton's death, and only took on its modern meaning of the scientific study of the human mind in the eighteenth century.[10] Burton believed that the best healer for a melancholic was a 'whole physician' (i.37); the idea of a specialist doctor for the mind would have been unknown to him, since the study of the mind, body, and soul was the province of physicians, philosophers, and theologians. Readers have often recognised in the descriptions of historical melancholy the hallmarks of conditions now known as depression, anxiety, bipolar disorder, and PTSD. For the most part, this book avoids drawing explicit connections with such conditions, for several reasons. Firstly, to do so runs the risk of making reductive and potentially damaging associations for modern readers. Moreover, retrospectively diagnosing diseases in past lives on the basis of limited information is not only difficult, but also a morally questionable enterprise. It denies the culturally situated nature of past and present understandings of the workings of mind and body. Lastly, perhaps substituting our new words for old detracts from the dignity of those who suffered, talked about, and treated mental disorders in the past. Oliver Sacks has said that 'to restore the human subject at the centre – the suffering, afflicted, fighting, human subject – we must deepen a case history to a narrative or tale: only then do we have a "who" as well as a "what", a real person, a patient, in relation to disease'. That task is often inaccessible when the records of Renaissance melancholic case histories are brief and when the identities of most patients are lost to us. Yet the history of melancholy also reveals much that is, in Sacks' words, 'richly human', and deserves to be taken on its own terms.[11] This book suggests that the words sufferers and healers of melancholy knew and used, and the ways they expressed the contours of human suffering, have much to teach us about their own habits of mind and perhaps – by reflection – our own.

PART 1

CAUSES

1

Sorrow and Fear

A Jew in France (saith Lodovicus Vives) came by chance over a dangerous passage or plank that lay over a brook, in the dark, without harm, the next day, perceiving what danger he was in, fell down dead. Many will not believe such stories to be true, but laugh commonly, and deride when they hear of them; but let these men consider with themselves, as Peter Bayrus illustrates it, if they were set to walk upon a plank on high, they would be giddy, upon which they dare securely walk upon the ground.

(Burton, *Anatomy*, i.256)

When we talk about melancholy in its modern sense, we usually understand it to mean a state of sadness, dejection, and introspection. Fear does not enter into our definitions of it.[1] In the Renaissance, however, to be melancholic was to live in fear. Anxiety, terror, sudden frights, and phobias were all seen as hallmarks of the disease, along with sorrow. In *The Anatomy of Melancholy*'s English predecessor, Timothy Bright's *Treatise of Melancholy* (1586), fear rather than sadness is the disease's defining characteristic: it is 'either a certain fearful disposition of the mind altered from reason, or else an humour of the body, commonly taken to be the only cause of reason by fear in such sort depraved'.[2]

In this chapter we will consider what makes sorrow and fear the inseparable companions of melancholy and how these two emotions can play complex roles in the workings – or failings – of human minds and bodies. Burton claims that they are like cousins or even sisters, so close is their relationship with one another and with the condition he has dedicated himself to exploring. Not only the principal causes of melancholy, they are also its defining symptoms: he quotes Hippocrates' claim that sorrow is 'the mother and daughter of melancholy', both the origin and the offspring of mental distress. These emotions 'beget one another, and tread in a ring' (i.259). A bereavement may lead to a lasting, unshiftable sorrow. A sudden fright may turn into a lifelong phobia.

Falling off a Log

The story Burton tells of the sixteenth-century Jewish Frenchman not only shows how strong the imagination can be, but also plays out an intriguing philosophical puzzle. A man puts his life at risk by crossing over a brook by night but, since he is unable to see, he cannot perceive the danger he is in. Instead, his perception comes after the event. The case is an unusual one – and so probably appealed to Burton – because normally fear is an emotion connected to something that is is yet to happen. Aristotle describes it as a 'sort of pain or agitation derived from the imagination of a future destructive or painful evil'.[3] But in this case, the man's fear is connected to an event that has already occurred.

Burton found the story in the writings of the Spanish humanist Juán Luís Vives (1492–1540) on the soul. Vives uses it to illustrate the notion that our imaginations function by making something present to us, whether that something is in the past, future, or is completely non-existent. Darkness robbed the Frenchman of the sensory information he needed to interpret the risk of walking along the plank, so his imagination supplied it instead (but only later, since he did not know what he was doing at the time). Burton removes one interesting detail in Vives' original account, that the man was returning home by night on his donkey and had drifted off to asleep. Whereas Vives' version has him unconscious, Burton makes him alert but unseeing. When he revisited the scene the next day, the man saw what he could not have done by night, and died of shock at what might have been. A fall from a height may have put his life at risk, but it was imagination that killed him.

Vives' Frenchman walked in a long line of people who crossed dangerous bridges. Even Burton acknowledges that there are those who will doubt whether it is true, probably knowing that 'the man who walked along a plank' was a centuries-old test-case for the nature of fear. Variations of the story exist in many forms. It may originate in the writings of the eleventh-century Persian philosopher and physician, Ibn Sina (Avicenna), who notes that a man can

> run fast on a plank of wood when it is put across a well-trodden path, but when it is put like a bridge over a chasm, he would hardly be able to creep over it. This is because he pictures to himself a fall so vividly that the natural power of the limbs accords with it.

The example was taken up by Western scholars interested in the mind's powers over the body. In his *Summa theologiae*, Thomas Aquinas follows Ibn Sina in remarking that 'because of his fear a man who sets out to walk across a plank high above the ground will easily fall'. But if the plank is lowered, he reasons, the man would be less likely to stumble and fall because he would not be afraid. 'Fear interferes with action', he concludes.[4]

Closer to Burton's time, in his 'Apology for Raymond Sebond' the French essayist Michel de Montaigne

(1533–92) has a more extreme idea for putting a medieval theory to practical experiment:

> Take a philosopher, put him in a cage made from thin wires set wide apart; hang him from one of the towers of Notre Dame de Paris. It is evident to his reason that he cannot fall; yet (unless he were trained as a steeplejack) when he looks down from that height he is bound to be terrified and beside himself.

We can test the limits of our reason without having to harm any philosophers, however:

> Take a beam wide enough to walk along: suspend it between two towers: there is no philosophical wisdom, however firm, which could make us walk along it just as we would if we were on the ground.[5]

Whether or not Vives' Frenchman really lived out (and died from) the thought experiment that Ibn Sina, Aquinas, and Montaigne all posed, his story contains in miniature the twin features of the many case histories in *The Anatomy of Melancholy*. On the one hand, it is curious, extreme, and hard to believe. On the other, it is a story with which we might identify. While retrospective fear certainly seems like an outlandish cause of death, everyone has experienced the physical effects of fright, such as a racing heartbeat and feeling short of breath. We may marvel or even laugh at these stories but – as Burton and Montaigne remind us – we would not be able to help feeling giddy if we were standing above the same precipice.

Terrors and Affrights

Sorrow and fear can cause melancholy when they are excessive in proportion to the object, when they come

FIGURE 1.1 Face of a frightened soldier (left); the human face in an animal state of fear (right). Etching by B. Picart, 1713, after Charles Le Brun (1619–90).

on too quickly, or when they become engrained. In the case of Vives' Frenchman, there was not time for his fear to become a longer-term condition because he was killed so suddenly. The fear he might have felt gradually, as he prepared to cross the plank, came upon him all at once the next day. Burton is fascinated by the phenomenon of terror, and moreover by the sheer power of the imagination to bring on extreme consequences: 'sometimes death itself is caused by force of phantasy', he remarks. 'I have heard of one that, coming by chance in company of him that was thought to be sick of the plague (which was not so), fell down suddenly dead' (i.256). But if not all cases are instantly fatal, they can certainly have unforeseen consequences.

Burton treats 'Terrors and Affrights Causes of Melancholy' differently from other kinds of fear. This is partly a question of degree – they are at the extreme end of the emotional spectrum – and partly because that severity makes for sudden and acute effects on the body and mind: 'Of all fears they are most pernicious and violent, and so suddenly alter the whole temperature of the body, move the soul and spirits, strike such a deep impression, that the parties can never be recovered, causing more grievous and fiercer melancholy' (i.335; see Figure 1.1). The cause might be an imminent danger, but it could just as well be a trick of the imagination.

Such was the case of the Swiss gentlewoman and the dead pig. Burton recounts a story from the casebooks of the physician Felix Platter of one of his patients, a lady from the city of Basle who happened to see a pig being butchered. A doctor (not Platter himself) was standing nearby and noticed how much the smell and sight of the pig's entrails was upsetting the woman. Not blessed with tact, he quipped that 'as that hog, so was she, full of filthy excrements'. At this discovery of what the insides of her own body looked and smelled like, she had an instant reaction which became a long-lasting one:

> she fell forthwith a-vomiting, was so mightily distempered in mind and body, that with all his art and persuasions, for some months after, he [Platter] could not restore her to herself again; she could not forget it, or remove the object out of her sight. (i.337)

As is often the case with melancholy, what might be for most people only a passing annoyance is, for one person, the trigger for long-term illness. Burton calls these 'our melancholy provocations' and warns readers who are tempted to be dismissive of them that we should not judge by how we might respond to the same stimulus. We cannot measure another person's suffering by our own reactions, 'for that which is but a flea-biting to one, causeth insufferable torment to another' (i.145).

While the melancholy brought on by shock, fear, and grief affects individuals in unpredictable ways, it can also assault whole populations. The 'terrors and affrights' which Burton records include the mental trauma brought on by cataclysmic events, the effects of which can be felt long after they have passed. On 30 December 1504, a terrible earthquake struck Bologna in Italy, one of many that the city has endured over the centuries. It started at eleven at night, forcing its citizens out into the streets. Among them was the humanist scholar Filippo Beroaldo, whose eye-witness account Burton uses as a source for the *Anatomy*. The whole city shook, Beroaldo recalls, and 'the people thought the world was at an end ... such a fearful noise it made, such a detestable smell, the inhabitants were infinitely affrighted, and some ran mad' (i.338).

While many were driven to wild distress by the terrifying events of that night, one or two bore more severe mental scars. Beroaldo tells the strange story of one citizen, Fulco Argelanus, 'a bold and proper man', who was 'so grievously terrified with it, that he was first melancholy, after doted, at last mad, and made away himself' (i.338). This description shows the way that mental illness was distinguished in the Renaissance, not so much by different types, as by degrees of severity: as Argelanus' state of mind deteriorated, he went from melancholy to dotage to madness, each successive name describing a more acute state. Melancholy verges into madness when the sufferer has lost all control of his or her reason. In his retelling of the story, Burton suppresses several details that were in Beroaldo's original account: that the man first attempted suicide by cutting his throat, and that he finally threw himself off a high building. A violent natural disaster leads to a violent personal tragedy, but one that in this case is the result of delayed mental trauma rather than immediate physical damage.

Earthquakes were notorious in the Renaissance for their powers to endanger not just the body but also the mind. One reason for this was the noxious vapours they produced. During earthquakes in Japan in 1596, witnesses reported both a terrible noise and a filthy smell, and at Fushimi 'many men were offended with headache, many overwhelmed with sorrow and melancholy' (i.338). As is so often the case with melancholy, outer and inner causes and symptoms were intertwined. The toxic fumes affected the victims' brains and gave them headaches, even as the horrors being witnessed terrified the imaginations. While the effects on them were immediate, the damage could become permanent: 'many times, some years following, they will tremble afresh at the remembrance, or conceit of such a terrible object, even all their lives long, if mention be made of it' (i.338).

Refrigerating Passions

Why are fear and sadness so dangerous and self-propagating to melancholics? The answer is partly down to their intrinsic nature. From antiquity onwards, philosophers classified fear and sorrow as passions. Also known in the Renaissance as affections or perturbations of the soul, passions are similar to what we would now call emotions, but the way that they were conceptualised by writers of the period reveals a far more fundamentally embodied sense of what it means for humans to feel. The passions stand between our inner motions (our willpower and cognition) and our outer motions (our hearing, seeing, etc.) and they share something with both our senses and our reason – but not equally. After all, Renaissance theorists note, animals as well as humans have passions, and animals have no reasoning ability. The Jesuit writer Thomas Wright describes human passions and senses as like naughty servants who are disobedient to their master, reason, and who pay far more attention to one another, as friends in league.[6] Over the centuries, there was much debate over how many passions there were – answers ranged between two and eleven – but the basic set classified by Aquinas is four: fear, sorrow, joy (or love), and hope. Two of them live in the present: joy and sorrow. Two are concerned with what is to come, which we either wish for or want to avoid: hope and fear. All the other passions derive from these four, among them anger, envy, pride, jealousy, avarice, and shame.

The passions are a common cause of melancholy because, just as the bad humours of the body can work upon the brain and damage it, so the passions can alter the body's humoral balance. The consequences can be severe: as Burton puts it, 'the mind most effectually works upon the body, producing by his passions and perturbations miraculous alterations, as melancholy, despair, cruel diseases, and sometimes death itself' (i.250). He describes the actions of the passions in visceral terms: 'giving way to these violent passions of fear, grief, shame, revenge, hatred, malice, etc., they are torn in pieces, as Actaeon was with his dogs, and crucify their own souls' (i.259). Those who fall prey to the passions are victims, but Burton's words also hint at their personal responsibility for what happens to them: they are not crucified by the passions, but crucify themselves.

The story of Vives' Frenchman shows just how extreme the actions of the passions can be, 'producing … death itself', as Burton puts it. These effects were deemed to be more severe in certain groups of people: women, for instance. Renaissance readers would probably have found significance in the fact that the Frenchman was Jewish (Vives himself was the son of *converso* parents, that is, Jews who converted to Christianity). In the *Anatomy* Burton records several cases from his medical sources of Jewish sufferers from melancholy, where their susceptibility to the passions is a defining feature. The Italian physician Giambattista da Monte (Montanus, 1488–1551) for instance, 'had a melancholy Jew to his patient; he ascribes this for a principal cause … he was easily moved to anger' (i.270). The antisemitic slur that Jewish people were prey to the passions – seen on stage in the avarice and rage of Shakespeare's Shylock – is written into Renaissance medical theorising about the mind's health.

What did it mean, precisely, to die of shock and fear? We might assume that the Frenchman's experience simply brought on a heart attack. But Renaissance medicine provides a far more elaborate theory of how fear and sorrow can affect the heart, which is the 'seat of all affections'. Drawing on Aristotelian ideas of perception, Burton and others explain that, when we experience something with our senses or remember it and our memory amplifies it into a cause of sorrow or fear, the imagination sends a message to the heart. Several things happen in turn. First, the imagination's messengers – known as the spirits – 'flock from the brain to the heart, by certain secret channels' (i.252), to tell it how to respond to the external threat or upset. Then the heart uses the bodily humours to carry out its orders to the rest of the body, and thus disrupts their normal flow. When we are frightened or sad, the heart draws to itself melancholy, the cold and wet humour, to 'help it' in trying to avoid what causes grief. And, as Burton puts it, this 'refrigerates the heart' (i.260). The body's whole temperature changes as a result. Fear and sorrow take heat from the body's outside and contract it inwards. This is why, when we are scared, we shiver as we do when we are cold.

In itself, this process is not necessarily bad. When our imagination interprets what we perceive correctly – say, if we see an angry bull on the loose and think of it attacking us and goring us to death – its message to the heart tells it to avoid the danger as quickly as possible. We turn cold as the humours and spirits within the body become disrupted from their normal tasks so that they all act in the service of fear. The bodily change is a rapid one, and it saves our lives if we run for cover (though if we 'freeze', it may well put us in worse danger). Yet Burton is emphatic that fear and sorrow are damaging not just to the heart but to the whole body. When the passions disturb our bodily humours, 'the spirits so confounded, the nourishment must needs be abated, bad humours increased, crudities and thick spirits engendered, with melancholy blood. The other parts cannot perform their functions, having the spirits drawn from them by vehement passion' (i.252). Hence why fear turns our stomach and loosens our bowels, why sorrow stops us eating and makes us turn pale.

This Ocean of Misery

> All fears, griefs, suspicions, discontents, imbonities, insuavities are swallowed up, and drowned in this Euripus, this Irish sea, this ocean of misery, as so many small brooks; ... I say of our melancholy man, he is the cream of human adversity, the quintessence, and upshot; all other diseases whatsoever, are but flea-bitings to melancholy in extent: 'Tis the pith of them all.
>
> (i.434)

In trying to describe what it feels like to be melancholic, Burton reaches for the appropriate words to describe the suffering. He even invents new ones: 'imbonities' is his own coinage (meaning 'unkindnesses', 'absences of

FIGURE 1.2 *Melancholy.* Anonymous, after Parmigianino (1524–90).

goodness').[7] We have had those flea-bitings before, as a comparison of other pains with melancholy's ('ocean' is another favourite Burtonian measure: in the *Anatomy* there are oceans of 'adversity', 'troubles', 'cares', and 'a stupendous, vast, infinite ocean of incredible madness and folly', i.274, 323; iii.154, 313). That melancholy is the quintessence of all diseases is also an acknowledgement of how far it participates in different experiences.

Just as a wide variety of different fears can stimulate a case of melancholy, so can different sorrowful contexts. One of them is the indefinable experience of malaise expressed by Antonio in the opening words of *The Merchant of Venice* – 'In sooth I know not why I am so sad' – and in which Melancholy as a personified figure is often depicted (see Figure 1.2). Yet that mysteriously causeless sorrow is not attributable to all melancholy cases.[8] In the common definition of melancholy cited by Burton (and others), the disease has 'for his ordinary companions fear and sadness, without any apparent occasion' (i.170). The emphasis should be on 'apparent', though: in many cases there is an occasion responsible for producing the passions of fear and sadness, but – if the sufferer survives their initial onslaught – the emotional experience becomes unmoored from its original circumstances.

The initial causes of melancholic sorrow are many and, to those who do not fully understand them, they might appear only minor. Burton spends some time discussing the damaging experience of being on the receiving end of cruel words: 'a bitter jest, a slander, a calumny pierceth deeper than any loss, danger, bodily pain or injury whatsoever', he remarks, and 'many men are undone by this means, moped, and so dejected, that they are never to be recovered'. These 'arrows', as he calls them (drawing on biblical imagery), stick in the flesh until the victim is incurably injured. This is especially wounding for those people who already tend towards melancholy, since they are sensitive and prone to misconstruing other people's meanings. If they hear something barbed or inconsiderate said of them, even in jest, 'they aggravate, and so meditate continually of it, that it is a perpetual corrosive, not to be removed till time wear it out' (i.341). The corporeal language Burton uses to describe this hurt is vivid. Even a moment of thoughtless cruelty can leave poison beneath the skin.

More tangible, environmental causes are responsible for the same condition. Burton expresses compassion for those forced to live in confinement: women in Spain, Italy, and Turkey who are forced to stay at home, for instance, or those under long prison sentences. Likewise, he mourns the miserable fate of the enslaved, among them the '30,000 Indian slaves at Potosi, in Peru' condemned to a life in the mines of 'perpetual drudgery, hunger, thirst, and stripes, without all hope of delivery!' (i.345). This is far from fashionable melancholy in the Ficinian mode. That Burton attributes 'heart-eating melancholy' to the enslaved and the poor, 'preyed upon by polling officers for breaking the laws, by their tyrannizing landlords, so flayed and fleeced by perpetual exactions, that … they cannot live' (i.352), shows the seriousness of his social purpose. The condition he analyses is inflicted not just by individual misfortune but by structures of power. Condemning this inhumane treatment, Burton is alert to the mental degradation caused by a life of hardship and persecution.

One of the things that these examples have in common is the lack or the loss of freedom. As Burton remarks, using a story from the physician Girolamo Cardano (1501–76), the power of restrictions lies more in their power to control us than in whether they make any difference to our actual behaviour:

Were we enjoined to go to such and such places, we would not willingly go: but being barred of our liberty, this alone torments our wandering soul that we may not go. A citizen of ours, saith Cardan, was sixty years of age, and had never been forth of the walls of the city of Milan; the prince hearing of it, commanded him not to stir out: being now forbidden that which all his life he had neglected, he earnestly desired, and being denied, *dolore confectus mortem, obiit*, he died for grief. (ii.173)

The pressure of physical, mental, and spiritual restrictions – whether self-imposed or enforced by others – typically occasions the sorrow which is, in turn, a major cause of melancholy, and which in the case of this man proved fatal.

Melancholy brings to light how much difference personal perspective makes to our responses to external circumstances. When Burton consoles his reader against loss of liberty, imprisonment, and exile, he draws attention to this very question:

> We are all prisoners. What is our life but a prison? We are all imprisoned in an island. The world itself to some men is a prison, our narrow seas as so many ditches, and when they have compassed the globe of the earth, they would fain go see what is done in the moon. (ii.173)

Burton never travelled beyond the shores of Britain (or at least so he tells us) and insular experience informs his idea of common imprisonment. His words might recall Hamlet, telling Rosencrantz and Guildenstern that 'Denmark's a prison', and saying that he 'could be bounded in a nutshell and count myself a king of infinite space, were it not that I have bad dreams'.[9] By contrast, the boundless curiosity to travel in an unrestricted way is, Burton hints, not morally neutral. Those men who have 'compassed the globe of the earth' and are still unsatiated have the tincture of Satan, who, when God asks him when he has come from, replies, 'From compassing the earth to and fro, and from walking in it' (Job 1:7).[10]

If melancholics desire unfettered freedom, they are also desiring beyond human powers.

Melancholy in Chains

Melancholy illness is not any upsetting reaction to an unpleasant event; rather it is a reaction that sticks and becomes a fixed habit. We have seen how captivity of one form or another causes unshiftable grief, and this also provides a compelling language for what it feels like to be melancholy. When someone becomes prey to the condition, the whole self is altered – body, mind, and soul – so that every small emotional disturbance has a disproportionate effect: 'And as it is with a man imprisoned for debt, if once in the jail, every creditor will bring his action against him, and there likely hold him' – that is, every person to whom he owes money brings a case against him and keeps him there – 'if any discontent seize upon a patient, in an instant all other perturbations … will set upon him, and then like a lame dog or broken-winged goose he droops and pines away' (i.146). Melancholy is both self-propagating and ensnaring.

The imagery of melancholic captivity is shared among Renaissance writers. Timothy Bright describes this process in similar terms to Burton. When a melancholic fears one thing, he fears everything, 'even as one condemned to death with undoubted expectation of execution, fearing every knock at the prison door, hath horror, though the messenger of pardon with knock require to be admitted and let in'.[11] Even good things may become alarming to the melancholic when the heart is overcome with present grief and fear of the future. And for the

Jesuit Thomas Wright, the passions 'keep the mind in a perpetual dungeon, and oppress it with continual fears, anxieties, sorrows' (i.420).[12]

This is why melancholy is so tormenting a malady, why sorrow and fear are both cause and symptom. An initial circumstance, whether serious or seemingly trivial, can provoke the settled condition that Burton calls habitual melancholy. One of his stories of this originates in the passion closely related to both sorrow and fear, shame, and is taken from the casebooks of the sixteenth-century Dutch physician Pieter van Foreest (Forestus, 1522–97):

A grave and learned minister, and an ordinary preacher at Alkmaar in Holland, was (one day as he walked in the fields for his recreation) suddenly taken with a lask [attack of diarrhoea] or looseness, and thereupon compelled to retire to the next ditch; but being surprised at unawares by some gentlewomen of his parish wandering that way, was so abashed, that he did never after show his head in public, or come into the pulpit, but pined away with melancholy. (i.263–4)

Like a broken-winged goose, the man was fatally debilitated by his experience. He became imprisoned in his own home, held captive by the shame of a single incident that came to define him.

In describing the workings of sorrow, Burton turns to a classical analogy: ''Tis the eagle without question, which the poets fained to gnaw Prometheus' heart' (i.259). The tortured Prometheus, chained to the rocks of the Caucasus for stealing fire from the gods (Figure 1.3), is a model for the grieving melancholic as a tortured heroic sufferer. In most versions of the Prometheus myth, it is his liver which the eagle eats while Prometheus is chained

FIGURE 1.3 Prometheus bound to a rock, his liver eaten by an eagle. Engraving by C. Cort (1566).

to rocks and which renews itself every night.[13] While the liver itself has an ancient association with emotions, Burton's alteration of the organ to the heart aligns the myth with the physiological workings of sorrow, attacking the heart.

There are two more occasions when Burton revisits the same myth as he attempts to describe what it is like to suffer from melancholy. One is at the beginning of his section on symptoms. He introduces the subject by recalling the shocking story of the Athenian painter Parrhasius, who bought an elderly slave from the captives of Philip of Macedon's war and 'put him to extreme torture and torment, the better by his example to express the pains and passions of his Prometheus, whom he was then about to paint'. He compares his own task to this: 'I need not be so barbarous, inhuman, curious, or cruel, for this purpose to torture any poor melancholy man; their symptoms are plain, obvious and familiar ... their grievances are too well known, I need not seek far to describe them' (i.382). Though the suffering produced by grief and fear might seem to be entirely within, Burton suggests that the evidence of it is as perceptible as Prometheus' torture is, written on his body.

On the other occasion when Burton visits the myth, it is to draw an even closer link: 'a melancholy man is that true Prometheus, which is bound to Caucasus; the true Tityus, whose bowels are still by a vulture devoured' (i.434). The torment of melancholy is as horrendous as any invented by the ancient gods. While the occasions that trigger it may be minor or even the matter of moments, its agony becomes as inescapable and perpetual as Prometheus', or that of the giant Tityos, condemned in Tartarus to a similar punishment.

That Burton uses the Prometheus myth as a metaphor for what melancholy feels like is a way of suggesting, not just the extremity of this torment, but the role that art and literature can play in articulating, and thus representing, suffering. While his catalogue of melancholy draws from the shelves of Renaissance medical textbooks, it also finds source material beyond casebooks and theory: in poetry, philosophy, the classics, and scripture. His writing interweaves the histories of real patients diagnosed as melancholic with stories and quotations from mythology and literature.

Burton does not distinguish between these types of source material because they all offer kinds of truth-telling. When he documents the effects of bereavement, for example, Burton can cite a range of examples from medical writings: the fifty-year-old man who was 'desperate upon his mother's death' and was cured by the physician Gabriello Fallopio, only to relapse many years later after the sudden death of his daughter, 'and could never be recovered'; Giambattista da Monte's patient, who was troubled with melancholy for many years after the loss of her husband. But he also quotes King David mourning the death of his son – 'O my dear son Absalom!' (cf. 2 Samuel 18:33) – and Niobe in Ovid's *Metamorphoses* (Figure 1.4), whose grief for the loss of her children was so great that 'the poets feigned her to be turned into a stone, as being stupefied through the extremity of grief' (i.360).

That Fallopio's and da Monte's patients had 'real' diagnoses, while Niobe's grief belongs only to myth and David's to ancient Hebrew history and the poetry of the Psalms, is irrelevant to Burton. Medical case histories may record incidents and examples, but they usually do not let sufferers speak, and one of the aims of the *Anatomy* is to bear witness to the scale and variety of melancholic suffering from the perspective of the sufferer, not just the physician. The passions of sorrow and fear which are at the

FIGURE 1.4 *Niobe and her Daughter*. Etching by F. Perrier, 1638.

root of melancholy may do their work through the imagination, yet it also takes an act of the imagination truly to empathise with those who suffer – and, perhaps, to find our own experiences reflected in melancholy's dark mirror.

In the next chapter, we continue to examine this 'compound mixed malady' (i.37) by considering in more depth how Renaissance medicine conceived of melancholy as a disease of body, mind, and soul, and by exploring some of the physical and visible traits of this disorder.

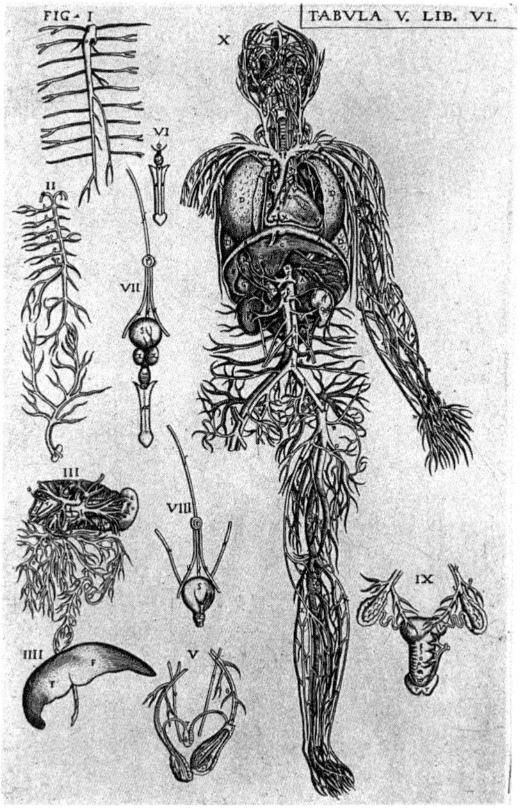

FIGURE 2.1 The venous and arterial system of the human body with internal organs and detail figures of the generative system. Engraving (1568).

2

Body and Mind

In 1549, the celebrated Paduan physician Giambattista da Monte treated the Earl of Montfort for a case of hypochondriacal melancholy. Nowadays, the term 'hypochondria' refers to an excessive anxiety that one has a serious medical condition. But in the sixteenth and seventeenth centuries, it had a different meaning: hypochondriacal melancholy was of a specific type that was located in the hypochondriac region, the middle region of the body just below the midriff, where the liver, spleen, and gallbladder reside. In Renaissance physiology, these organs comprise the central system both for producing the humours and for refining them from the nutrition that the body takes in. In the Earl of Montfort's case, his belly was too cold while his liver was too hot. He was suffering from pustules and ulcers. He had indigestion and bad wind. And he was experiencing the gloom and sadness which are the typical accompaniments of melancholic disease.

This illustrious patient suffered from a chronic condition that revealed itself as much in the body as in the mind, and his doctor treated him accordingly. Da Monte's aim in treatment was both to restore his body to health and to quieten his spirits, prompting him towards contentment and tranquillity. Therefore he advised his patient to leave the royal court and all the troubles, jealousies, ambition, and politicking that went along with it. He should avoid eating pork and fish; he should drink white wine; he should live in a pleasant house with good air (conveniently, the Montfort family's ancestral home lies on the north shore of Lake Constance). He should refrain from sex, though since the patient was not keen on the idea of total abstinence, the doctor compromised and asked him to moderate his sexual activity – and never on a full stomach. The doctor also devised a purge, with ingredients including flowers from the golden shower tree (an ancient purgative remedy in Eastern and Western medicine), rhubarb, and spices.[1]

Thus Giambattista da Monte treated his patient for complex disorder of body, mind, and spirit with therapies that responded to the same. The case of the Earl of Montfort is one that Robert Burton refers to a number of times in the *Anatomy* and reveals how closely and intricately Renaissance physicians thought that the body and mind worked together. On the one hand, emotional disturbances could cause bodily illnesses. On the other, bodily diseases could 'affect the soul by consent' (i.374). Burton mentions cases where patients degenerated into melancholy states after contracting an ague, or plague, or syphilis, or epilepsy. And likewise, mental disturbance could often lead to physical sickness.

In this chapter we shall explore the variety of ways in which body and mind interact in Renaissance melancholy. These days, we commonly describe physical ailments that have psychological origins as psychomatic, a word that combines the Greek words for mind or spirit – psyche – and body. The word is a nineteenth-century coinage – the *Oxford English Dictionary* finds its first usage in Samuel Taylor Coleridge – and has only been used in a medical context since the early twentieth century.[2] Yet the ancient Galenic medical tradition that Giambattista da Monte, Robert Burton, and their contemporaries followed provided a highly sophisticated understanding of how physical and mental health were intertwined, and of how one could affect the other. It was not only obvious to them, but also thoroughly logical according to medical theory, that a stomach complaint could cause a chronic low mood or that long-term sadness could break out in a skin rash. As we have seen, the Earl of Montfort's hypochondriacal melancholy had physical features as well as mental ones; indigestion, headaches, and vertigo were all recognised symptoms of the disease.

Burton uses a musical image to explain how the body works upon the mind: 'as a lute out of tune; if one string or one organ be distempered, all the rest miscarry' (i.375), so something wrong in one part of the body can affect the whole person. 'Distemperature' is a term commonly used in Renaissance medical writing which points to the heart of theories about the self. If the string of a musical instrument is distempered, it has slid out of tune. If a body or a part of the body is distempered, it has lost its fundamental balance: the perfect combination of cold, heat, moisture, and dryness that it needs to function properly.

What we nowadays mean by bodily temperature – in other words, how hot or cold it is – is only one element of the Renaissance idea of temperature: how well ordered or otherwise the body and mind are, and how the humours combine to contribute towards a person's distinctive features, personal character, and overall disposition. Renaissance selfhood and emotional experience are far more than simple products of the humoral body;

nonetheless, their constructions are underpinned by a sophisticated and complex theory of the interrelationship of body and mind.[3] The Earl of Montfort's anxious and downcast state of mind was not simply the result of humoral imbalance and intestinal gas. It was also caused by the mental strain of life at court, and the therapies da Monte prescribed took account of this. We shall consider first the matter of melancholy itself and how it could be inherited; then some Renaissance ideas about how melancholy appeared in the visible features of sufferers; and we will explore the multiple varieties of melancholic disease that could be produced by 'adustion' or corruption of the humours. Finally, we will turn to the colour of black bile as it reveals itself not only in individuals, but nations and peoples.

The Matter of Melancholy

Everyone has melancholy within them, but not everyone suffers from it: that is the classical humoral theory upon which Burton's understanding of the disease depends. The four humours are fluids in the body which each have different qualities and which work together to support life. We know what some of them look like, most obviously blood: the hot, moist humour that nourishes and strengthens the body. Blood performs the role of keeping different parts of the body in communication with one another through the veins and arteries (see Figure 2.1) because it is a channel for the spirits: vapours that are the instruments of the soul and which form 'a common tie or medium between the body and the soul' (i.148). Phlegm, likewise, is sometimes visible. The cold and moist humour, its job is both to nourish the body and to keep the moving parts lubricated, such as the tongue through saliva. The other two, dry humours are more hidden within the body. Choler or yellow bile, hot and dry, helps to preserve the natural heat of the body, aid the senses, and to expel excrements. Finally there is melancholy or black bile, 'cold and dry, thick, black, and sour … a bridle to the other two hot humours, blood and choler, preserving them in the blood, and nourishing the bones' (i.148). We do not normally see melancholy as we would phlegm, but its presence might be detected in a blackened stool or dark-coloured blood.

The humours maintain a careful balancing act to regulate the body's temperature and to offset one another. Galen taught that there are three states of life: there is health, sickness, and a medium, neutral state between these two contraries. Most people fall into the middle category, and very few can be deemed fully healthy. As Burton's contemporary John Donne puts it in his poem *The First Anniversary*:

There is no health: physicians say that we
At best enjoy but a neutrality.
And can there be worse sickness than to know
That we are never well, nor can be so? (lines 91–4)[4]

A neutral state of health simply means an absence of sickness, while in that elusive, ideally healthy body, the humours work in perfect harmony with one another.

The humours have several correspondences. The inner workings of the human body are a miniature form of the whole cosmos, and the four humours are linked to the four elements: blood and air, phlegm and water, choler and fire, melancholy and earth. So the whole world mirrors what is going on within a single human being, and vice versa. The humours also correspond to the phases of human life, and this explains one facet of why not only our bodies but our attitudes and behaviour change as we get older. Young people abound in natural heat. As a result they are prone to choler or hot-headedness, easily losing their temper; they are energetic and more prone to lust and sensuosity. Healthy young people have colourful cheeks, a sign of a sanguine temperament (where blood predominates). With age, the body's finite stores of what is known as the *humidum radicale* – radical moisture – become depleted. The *humidum radicale* is the vital force that gives us energy. We naturally lose it as we get older, but our habits may use it up it faster. Frequent sex, drunkenness, anything that causes us to perspire all heat the body and expend moisture, of which the body only has a limited amount. This is one reason why the Earl of Montfort was instructed to moderate (if he could not abstain from) his sexual activity. Illness depletes the *humidum radicale* too, fevers in particular because they cause sweats and frequent changes in the body's temperature.

As people get older, their heat and moisture diminish and hence their humoral dispositions become drier and colder. According to Renaissance medical theory, this is evident in the fact that old people are wrinkly. And as an inevitable result of this drying and cooling process, the humour black bile is 'superabundant' in them. The common accompaniments of old age – physical inaction and weakness, loneliness, aches and pains, griefs – are part and parcel of the melancholy state:

After seventy years (as the Psalmist saith [Psalms 90:10]) "all is trouble and sorrow"; and common experience confirms the truth of it in weak and old persons, especially such as have lived in action all their lives, had great employment, much business, much command, and many servants to oversee, and leave off *ex abrupto* [abruptly], as Charles the Fifth did to King Philip, resign up all on a sudden; they are overcome with melancholy in an instant. (i.210)

Perhaps Burton knew the Holy Roman Emperor Charles V's abdication speech of 1555, which is distinctly melancholy in tone: in the version recorded by his biographer Prudencio de Sandoval, Charles says that he has given up his throne to his son Philip only reluctantly after a long and arduous reign, and mentions 'that nothing troubled him so much as leaving of [his subjects], but that his want of health rendered him incapable of being longer serviceable to them'.[5] A comparable example of someone who retired *ex abrupto* is King Lear, whose rapid mental deterioration comes as he divests himself of the cares of state. Both a lack of occupation and diminishing strength take their toll on the mind and the body. Burton follows Philipp Melanchthon in claiming it 'as an undoubted truth … that old men familiarly dote … for black choler' (i.210).

Though everyone who lives to a certain age eventually succumbs to melancholy, some people are predisposed to it from birth. Melancholy is a hereditary disease. Where we might understand this in genetic terms, Burton and his contemporaries held that a person's humoral constitution was transmitted through the bodily fluids of parents. The sixteenth-century French physician Jean Fernel argues that any illness that affects the father at the time of conception can be passed on through his semen to the child.[6] So, if a father is inclined towards an excess of black bile, the fluid he ejaculates will be of the same condition, and will form a foetus that is similarly inclined to melancholy.

Since older people are prone to melancholy, it is logical that, as the Dutch physician Lieven Lemmens (Lemnius, 1505–68) notes, 'old men beget most part wayward, peevish, sad, melancholy sons, and seldom merry' (i.213). Likewise, maternal blood can pass on infirmities. If a woman conceives a child during menstruation, that might result in a sickly child; or, to put it another way, if a child is born sickly, one explanation for this is that it was conceived during the mother's period. And even behaviour at the time of conception might affect the child's mind. Burton cites medical authorities who warn that those who have sex on a full stomach, or while drunk, or when they have a migraine are apt to conceive children who are infirm and melancholic.

Such is the intimate relationship between mind and body in Renaissance medical theory that the influence of parents is seen to go even further, imprinting upon their children the stamp of their own mental dispositions. The force of the imagination – especially the female imagination, women being more impressionable according to Galenic theory – can affect the development of the foetus. Thus one explanation for a disability – disconcerting to us – places responsibility on the mother; if she has a fright during pregnancy, her child might be deformed, while 'if a great-bellied woman see a hare, her child will often have an hare-lip' (i.215). This perceived effect could even be consciously manipulated. Burton tells the story of a Greek man who was ugly but who wanted to have a 'good brood of children'. So he bought the most beautiful pictures money could buy to hang in his chamber, 'that his wife by frequent sight of them, might conceive and bear such children'. One wonders whether the reasoning ever provided a convenient excuse for a woman whose children bore no resemblance to her husband, though Burton does not cast any doubt on the truth of Lieven Lemmens' claim that 'if a woman ... at the time of her conception think of another man present or absent, the child will be like him' (i.254–5).

The Melancholy Look

Both physical and mental attributes may be passed on through inheritance (though Renaissance theory allows for the possibility that it sometimes skips a generation), and each person is born with a humoral predisposition that affects their character. Those with a tendency towards an abundance of yellow bile are typically quick-tempered, otherwise known as choleric or bilious. Those rich in blood are sanguine, cheerful and sociable. An abundance of phlegm is associated with a laid-back, stolid temperament and slowness to rise to the bait: a phlegmatic personality. Those with a predominance of melancholy are intelligent and often scholarly, inclined to brooding solitude, but they do not necessarily suffer from melancholy as an illness.

These are the basic contours of the four humours, but the reality is often far more complex. More than one humour can predominate in a body at the same time and these work in combination, in the same way that primary colours blend into a spectrum of different shades. Different proportions might lead to a whole range of emotional dispositions. For example, someone who has a larger proportion of both blood and melancholy than the other two humours may be cheerful, bright in outlook and in mental capacity, while also being introspective.

Such a man was the French essayist Michel de Montaigne (1533–92). When describing himself in 'On Presumption', he notes that

my build is tough and thick-set, my face is not fat but full; my complexion is between the jovial and the melancholic, moderately sanguine and hot;

Unde rigent setis mihi crura, et pectora villis;

[Whence my hairy legs and my hirsute chest;]

my health is sound and vigorous and until now, when I am well on in years, rarely troubled by illness.[7]

Montaigne's self-portrait helpfully draws out important strands of humoral theory. He characterises his complexion – that is, his overall temperament – as a meeting-point between two humours. Though they have opposed qualities, blood being wet and hot while melancholy is dry and cold, these do not cancel one another out. Instead, they incline him towards cheerfulness and sharp intelligence. These two humours do not make him unwell, since they coexist in a stable balance. In another essay he does mention a spell of 'distempered' health: 'it was a melancholy humour (and therefore a humour most inimical to my natural complexion) brought on by the chagrin caused by the solitary retreat I plunged myself into a few years ago, which first put into my head this raving concern with writing'.[8]

Rather like Burton, Montaigne treats his writing as symptomatic of melancholic imbalance, a form of madness. But for him it is not one that comes naturally, since his predisposition is towards a healthy, sanguine temperament.

For Montaigne, his humoral state goes hand in hand with his physical appearance. His stocky build, his body hair, and his full face are signs of a healthy, moderately sanguine complexion. These elements contribute towards – though are by no means limited to – the self that he explores throughout his essays. It is interesting to note, by way of aside, that the English word 'complexion' has narrowed from its earlier Galenic meaning of the proportions of the humours in the body that make up a person's overall temperament to its modern usage, the colour and texture of the skin. For Montaigne, Burton, and their contemporaries, the complexion of the skin was only one, external indicator of the body's whole constitution.

Inner and outer states correspond to one another, and the disease of melancholy can be written not only onto how someone feels and behaves, but also onto how they look. Burton draws on two millennia of textbooks to catalogue the visible symptoms of melancholic disorder. According to the ancient Greek writings of the Father of Medicine, Hippocrates, melancholics are

> lean, withered, hollow-eyed, look old, wrinkled, harsh, much troubled with wind and a griping in their bellies, or belly-ache, belch often, dry bellies and hard, dejected looks, flaggy beards, singing of the ears, vertigo, light-headed, little or no sleep, and that interrupt, terrible and fearful dreams.

André du Laurens, physician to the French King Henri IV, adds that melancholics experience 'a kind of itching …

on the superficies of the skin, like a flea-biting sometimes' (i.383).

The contrast between melancholy as a fashionable aristocratic condition of the sixteenth century and melancholy as a chronic disease is a wide one. Those young Elizabethan men who had themselves painted in the voguish posture of melancholy – black clothing, a pale and serious expression, and standing half in shadow – bear little resemblance to the less attractive vision of the condition conjured by medical writers of the same period. And they would probably be less than keen to affect the many bodily symptoms Burton lists, including 'wind, palpitation of the heart, short breath, plenty of humidity in the stomach ... Their excrements or stool hard, black to some, and little' (i.384). In its bodily manifestations alone, the illness of melancholy was hardly to be welcomed.

Unnatural Melancholy

We have seen what happens when one humour which naturally occurs in the body becomes excessive. When melancholy abounds, it may make the body become distempered: unbalanced and diseased. But one of the curious aspects of melancholy as a disease is that it does not only derive from the humour of the same name. Burton quotes the sixth-century Roman Alexander of Tralles on the subject: 'there is not one cause of this melancholy, nor one humour which begets, but divers diversely intermixed, from whence proceeds this variety of symptoms' (i.399). A more extreme and dangerous form of melancholy can arise when any one of the four humours becomes adust: that is, when it comes burnt and corrupt. This is known as 'unnatural melancholy' because it does not derive from a humour in its natural state but rather from one that has blackened, which makes it resemble the original form and colour of melancholy.

As the physician Timothy Bright describes the process, when the body becomes too hot – for instance, when the liver becomes overheated, as it did in the Earl of Montfort's case – then the natural humours may become 'burned as it were into ashes in comparison of humour, by which the humour of like nature being mixed, turneth it into a sharp lye [an acrid, excremental fluid]: sanguine, choleric, or melancholic, according to the humour thus burned, which we call by name of melancholy'.[9] These adust humours behave in different ways from their natural forms. Generally they cause harm not only in themselves but also by giving off foul vapours that rise to the brain. These vapours interfere with thoughts, stir passions, and corrupt the imagination. Not everyone agreed that all four humours could create unnatural melancholy. Some medical writers (including Galen and, following him, Bright) excluded phlegm because that humour is white, and how can white become black? But Burton finds enough support to argue that it can. Adustion produces a range of melancholic states, each of which resembles the humour from which it derives.

Phlegm adust is certainly the rarest kind of melancholy. It stirs up 'dull symptoms, and a kind of stupidity, or impassionate hurt' (i.400). Because phlegm is the cold and wet humour associated with the element of water (Figure 2.2), melancholics with phlegm adust are drawn to ponds, pools, and rivers. They like to spend a lot of time fishing, but they may also fear water and have dreams that they are drowning. Unlike the typical melancholic who is thin, withered, and restless, these tend to be fat and sleepy. They have an abundance of bodily fluids: they cry a lot, spit a lot, are troubled with rheums (mucus and watery secretions). They may also have delusions of a liquid kind: Burton cites the case treated by the sixteenth-century Spanish physician Cristóbal de Vega of a patient who believed that he was a cask of wine.

Those whose melancholy comes from choler adust, on the other hand, are aggressive and short-tempered. They are 'bold and impudent, and of a more hairbrain disposition, apt to quarrel and think of such things, battles, combats, and their manhood; furious, impatient in discourse, stiff, irrefragable in their tenents; and if they be moved,

FIGURE 2.2 *Phlegmaticus*. Engraving by Raphael Sadler (1583).

most violent, outrageous, ready to disgrace, provoke any, to kill themselves, and others'. By contrast to those with phlegm adust, choleric melancholics sleep very little. They are fierce and adventurous, and their melancholy can easily threaten to degenerate into full madness. One of the more exotic symptoms of this kind of melancholy is that sufferers can fall into fits where they speak all kinds of languages they have not been taught. One case of a sufferer from choler adust was an Italian who could 'make Latin verses when the moon was combust' – that is, at its closest point to the sun – but was 'otherwise illiterate' (i.401).

The illness that arises from blood adust is the exception to the general rule that melancholy is usually accompanied by 'fear and sadness, without any apparent occasion' (i.170). Sanguine melancholics instead are merry people who laugh a great deal and enjoy singing and dancing. Nonetheless, this manner can erupt into more extreme behaviour, a sign that they are distempered in their humours. Burton recounts a story from a continental medical history of a rural man called Brunsellius who was subject to sanguine melancholy. While he was in church listening to a sermon, he saw a woman fall off a bench, half-asleep. Most of the people who saw the incident laughed, 'but he for his part was so much moved, that for three whole days after he did nothing but laugh, by which means he was much weakened, and worse a long time following' (i.401). Burton's own literary persona of Democritus Junior has some kinship with him, taking after the Greek philosopher who was disposed to laughing in a 'merry madness' ('*hilare delirium*', i.400).

Like those who are predisposed towards a healthy, sanguine temperament, those who suffer from sanguine melancholy are ruddy-cheeked, yet the indicators of illness can be read in their features and their behaviour. They have a high colour and a tendency towards redness in the veins of the eyes. Because blood adust tends to overheat the brain, they are subject to delusions. While they enjoy the theatre, they might also imagine that they can see or hear plays. Aristotle tells the story of a man who would sit as if he were at the theatre, 'now clap his hands, and laugh, as if he had been well pleased with the sight' (i.400). But it is also sanguine melancholics that Aristotle might have meant when he asked why those who excel in philosophy, politics, poetry or the arts are so often melancholic'.[10] At least, that is what the French physician André du Laurens supposed, since sanguine melancholic are often deeply learned, witty, intellectually sharp people.

Finally, there is melancholy adust itself. When black bile becomes corrupted, all of its natural tendencies become more concentrated – a kind of melancholy squared. So sufferers are not only habitually solitary, but may become unable to bear the company of others and suspicious of everyone. Not merely gloomy, they become preoccupied with death, dreaming of graves and corpses. Their fearfulness becomes heightened into wild phobias. And they commonly experience hallucinations of a dark kind: they may become convinced that they see dead people or can talk with devils; they may even believe that they are dead themselves.

The Colour of Melancholy

We have seen that any one of the four humours can cause melancholy when they burn and corrupt, and that it is melancholy's blackness, in part, which defines its many permutations. The fourteenth-century medical writer Gentile da Foligno had a friend who suffered from melancholy adust and became convinced that a 'a black man in the likeness of a soldier' (i.402) was following him about wherever he went. There are several stories of 'black men' appearing to melancholics in the *Anatomy* and it is worth pausing to explore their meaning. We should still be cautious in how we interpret the adjective 'black' here: the Latin phrase that Burton translates here is 'militem nigrum', and the colour more probably refers to the soldier's armour or uniform. Similarly, when Burton mentions another example of melancholics who believe that they see and talk with 'black men' (i.402), he also quotes the Latin original in which they are 'monachos nigros'; that is, the 'black monks' of the Benedictine order. Here it is their clothing that is black rather than their skin.

But why do melancholics have delusions that they see black-robed Benedictine monks rather than the white-robed Carthusians? The standard explanation is that they are frightened by spectacles of an exterior blackness that is also within them. The medical rationale comes from optical theory, Burton explains:

> as he that looketh through a piece of red glass judgeth everything he sees to be red, corrupt vapours mounting from the body to the head, and distilling again from thence to the eye, when they have mingled themselves with the watery crystal which receiveth the shadows of things to be seen, make all things appear of the same colour, which remains in the humour that overspreads our sight, as to melancholy men all is black, to phlegmatic all white, etc. (i.425)

So visual perception becomes projection outwards of inner gloom, the condensed vapours of black bile forming a kind of melancholy contact lens. Melancholics quite literally see a darkness.

In the poem that prefaces the *Anatomy*, 'The Author's Abstract of Melancholy', Burton voices the alternating states of being both delighted and afflicted with the disease. One of the stanzas is about auditory and visual illusions:

Methinks I hear, methinks I see
Ghosts, goblins, fiends; my phantasy
Presents a thousand ugly shapes,
Headless bears, black men, and apes,
Doleful outcries, and fearful sights,
My sad and dismal soul affrights.
  All my griefs to this are jolly,
  None so damn'd as Melancholy. (i.12)

The 'black men' who are the object of terror for this melancholic are supernatural creatures, the phrase being a colloquial term for an evil spirit or bogeyman.[11] Nonetheless, the modern racial connotation is not entirely irrelevant, for the colour of these phantoms is part of an ideological construction of a feared other. Renaissance medical theory combines melancholy's material form and effects with racialised fear and hostility constructed by Europeans.

Just as the black humour affects the sufferer's perception of others, real or unreal, so it also makes their own melancholy visible to others. One of the hallmarks of natural melancholy – that is, the kind that comes from an excess of the same humour – is a black colour in the face (i.208). Those who suffer from it by inheritance may be born with a dark complexion, or darkening of the features may come on during a period of illness. As we have seen, other humoral types can result in different appearances: sanguine melancholics might have red faces, for instance. As this suggests, Renaissance medicine allows for the idea that physical complexion and even skin colour are not necessarily fixed, and may respond to changes in humoral constitution or even be manipulable.

Humoral theory challenges ideas of otherness even as it reinforces and upholds racial prejudices. A white European melancholic may be terrified of a 'black man' he sees, while that other figure is simultaneously the projection of a blackness that is within him. And the characteristics of different humoral types do not just run in families, but also across countries and ethnicities. The sixteenth-century French jurist and political writer Jean Bodin makes a direct connection between dark skin colour and the fact that melancholy is a black humour, claiming that those who live in southern countries are most subject to it. They are more cruel and violent, he argues, and also more lustful, which he sees as the result of 'spongious melancholy'. A hot climate makes for a larger number of mad men than in the north; Fez, Morocco, and Granada in Spain are particularly prone to it.

At the same time, in the tradition of the pseudo-Aristotelian *Problems*, people from southern countries are also characterised as wise, contemplative, skilled in the arts, and philosophically inclined: the hot sun of Egypt and Ethiopia is a purifying force that produces peoples who enquire into the secrets of nature and excel at mathematics. By contrast, Bodin argues, the climate of northern countries makes people more inclined to be phlegmatic: cold and dull, chaste, unsubtle, less sharp, but better at obeying and maintaining the law.[12] Though connections between humoral types and perceived racial characteristics were common in the period, there was not a full agreement about how they worked. Burton follows Bodin in some respects, but also cites other authorities who claim that people from northern climes are more liable to natural melancholy because the weather is cold and dry, especially near the North Pole (i.239).

To modern eyes, Burton's views on race and health can appear both forward-thinking and deeply discomforting. In a rare revelation of his own view – rather than of those of his books – he says,

> And sure, I think, it hath been ordered by God's especial providence, that in all ages there should be (as usually there is) once in six hundred years, a transmigration of nations, to amend and purify their blood, as we alter seed upon our land … to alter for our good our complexions, which were much defaced with hereditary infirmities, which by our lust and intemperance we had contracted. (i.212–13)

On the one hand, Burton suggests that migration is good for us. It is medically beneficial for altering entrenched humoral complexions and disrupting the associated bad habits of individual nations. The fact that Burton is writing six hundred years after the Norman invasion prompts the idea that another invasion might do Britain good and would even be divinely ordained. But on the other, his language of transmigration and purification also hints at ethnic cleansing, while his example of successful migration is the 'inundation of those northern Goths and Vandals' across Europe and beyond; as Mary Floyd-Wilson points out, it is a racialist notion of vigorous northern blood which Burton sees as necessary in order to strengthen the English.[13] By invoking God's special providence, he is calling on the same justification that colonisers used to violent ends in the Americas. The periodic invasion of England by other northern Europeans, he argues, was good for making its inhabitants become as healthy as 'those poor naked Indians are generally at this day, and those about Brazil .... free from all hereditary diseases or other contagion, whereas without help of physic they live commonly 120 years or more' (i.213). But he has nothing to say here about the current effects of transmigration on the health of those indigenous people, even though elsewhere he condemns the murder of millions of West Indians by Spanish invaders, documented in horrifying detail by Bartolomé de las Casas (i.58–9).

Melancholy in the Renaissance was deep-rooted in bodies both individually and collectively. Writers from the period used humoral theory to buttress cultural and racial stereotypes, where geography and climate predetermined characteristic types of behaviour. Burton's larger project is to show 'that all the world is mad, that it is melancholy, dotes' (i.39), and global melancholy encompasses the wide variety of sick bodies in their infinite variety of cases on display. In the next chapter, we shall see that melancholy is seen to work at a higher level still: in the stars.

FIGURE 3.2 An artist painting a woman with a hand mirror and the devil; representing the faculty of the imagination. Engraving (seventeenth century).

3
The Supernatural

In 1571, a fifteen-year-old girl in Leuven fell ill with strange and disturbing symptoms. Katherine Gualter was the daughter of a cooper and was usually in good health, with a temperament that inclined towards an equal mixture of the melancholy and sanguine humours. She had recently started her monthly periods. One day, Katherine ate a cake that had been given to her by a local woman with a bad reputation. She found it painful to swallow and afterwards she complained of strange stomach pains, exhaustion, dizziness, and nausea. Her symptoms suggested that she had been poisoned.

As the days wore on, her pains got worse rather than better. Soon she was experiencing fevers and breathlessness, then started to act violently towards herself. She had convulsions so severe that four men could not hold her down, throwing herself off her bed onto the ground. She turned black in the face, looking like someone that had been strangled. Her parents called on the services of not one but several physicians. Among them was their eminent neighbour: Cornelius Gemma, Professor of Medicine at the University of Leuven.

What Gemma saw first-hand was unlike any other medical case he had ever witnessed. One of his fellow doctors thought she had worms, but that transpired to be something of an understatement: after one fit of particularly severe stomach cramps, Katherine excreted a live eel, one and a half foot long. The eel was put in a basin and splashed about, but after they killed and dissected it, its body mysteriously vanished. Soon afterwards she started to vomit every day for two weeks, expelling twenty-four pounds of water each time. She then brought up other substances: large balls of hair, 'enough to have stuffed whole dozens of tennis balls'; pigeon dung; pieces of wood and parchment, some of them inscribed with mysterious markings; a black substance like coals; two pounds of pure blood; stones; bones, pieces of hair, and copper.[1]

The case history of Katherine Gualter falls across the boundaries of Renaissance medicine, and opens up questions about the complex relationship between physiology and supernatural causes of melancholy that we will explore throughout this chapter. Cornelius Gemma was a polymath, expert in astrology and cosmology as well as medical studies. He was as interested in natural prodigies, ghostly apparitions, and sun haloes as he was in plague outbreaks. When he attended the girl, he took her medical history and noted her humoral constitution and other significant factors. That she was a girl coming into sexual maturity (an age-old trope still familiar to us from any number of horror films) was an important factor in her condition; as we will see in Chapter 5, the menstrual cycle was thought to be connected with melancholy. Gemma's account suggests that he and others thought the devil was at work in the girl, and Robert Burton includes the story in his discussion of how spirits and devils cause melancholy, alongside the story of the nun who 'did eat a lettuce without grace or signing it with the sign of the cross, and was instantly possessed' (i.201).

In Burton's retelling, Cornelius Gemma and his medical colleagues 'could do no good on her by physic, but left her to the clergy' (i.201). Yet, in Gemma's own version of events, his response was much less clear-cut. He did hand her over to priests, who said prayers over her and conducted a mass, but he also treated her medically for the physical symptoms he observed: a swollen stomach; anorexia (a word which in that time referred simply to want of appetite rather than to a recognised psychological condition); dropsy; a hernia she had after so much vomiting. Doctors and priests worked together patiently over several months to cure a girl whose suffering they saw as both demonically induced and the result of natural causes.

Cosmic Illness

Though Burton only uses the story of Katherine Gualter to illustrate supernatural causes, throughout the *Anatomy* he is emphatic that melancholy is a mixed condition. Himself an ordained minister of the Church of England rather than a doctor of medicine, Burton justifies his whole project of writing about melancholy by arguing that it is 'a disease of the soul on which I am to treat, and as much appertaining to a divine as to a physician; and who knows not what an agreement there is betwixt these two professions?' Priests are 'spiritual physician[s]', treating the vices and passions of the soul just as doctors apply remedies to bodily diseases:

> Now this being a common infirmity of body and soul, and such a one that hath as much need of a spiritual as a corporal cure, I could not find a fitter task to busy myself about, a more apposite theme, so necessary, so commodious, and generally

concerning all sorts of men, that should so equally participate of both, and require a whole physician. A divine in this compound mixed malady can do little alone, a physician in some kinds of melancholy much less, both make an absolute cure. (i.37)

An English Protestant clergyman such as Burton would be unlikely to conduct exorcisms on suspected demoniacs, but prayer and spiritual counsel were intrinsic parts of his ministry.

Burton is quite typical of his age in regarding God as the first general cause of disease, 'for the punishment of sin, and satisfaction of His justice' (i.178). The Old Testament furnishes him with stories of people whom God has struck down with disease, and specifically melancholy: the Israelites, who rebelled against God and were brought down with 'heaviness of heart' (Psalms 107:12); King Saul, who was vexed with an evil spirit (1 Samuel 16:14); Nebuchadnezzar, who ate grass like an ox (Daniel 5:21). So all those who are ill must look to God first for mercy: 'as it is with them that are wounded with the spear of Achilles, He alone must help; otherwise our diseases are incurable, and we not to be relieved' (i.179–80).

A further supernatural cause is found in the stars. They are literally supernatural – above nature – because in the geocentric universe they occupy the celestial sphere beyond the moon. All nature that exists in the sublunary sphere (that is, below the moon) is liable to change, corruption, and mortality; everything above it is permanent and unalterable. So the stars and planets move in their fixed courses around the earth and, as they do, they influence all that goes on there. It may seem surprising that a clergyman is willing to countenance astrology but Burton's stance was common in his day. 'If thou shalt ask me what I think', he says, typically quoting someone else in his answer, the stars 'do incline, but not compel … and so gently incline, that a wise man may resist them'. For Burton and many of his contemporaries, to believe their influence on humans is simply to recognise that the heavens are God's instrument and his 'great book, whose letters are the stars' (i.206).

Paracelsus (1493–1541), the German physician and alchemist whose medical theories presented the only major alternative to mainstream Galenic medicine in Burton's time, stresses that knowledge of the heavens is essential to any understanding of the cause or cure of diseases, even toothache. Certain planets have a special influence over types of human behaviour and bodily health. Saturn is the planet of melancholy – from whence a saturnine disposition – and makes one prone to sorrow, fearfulness, solitude, and silence. Jupiter influences a sanguine, jovial disposition and makes people ambitious. But just as the humours are normally mixed, so the celestial bodies work their influence together, sometimes in a hostile or warring manner. The cheerful melancholy of blood adust comes from the conjunction of Saturn and Jupiter in Libra. The planets Mars and Mercury are also significant, Mars because it corresponds to choler and inclines people towards violence and aggresion, and Mercury because those under its influence are contemplative, subtle thinkers, such as poets and philosophers (i.207–8, 398). The positions of Mercury, Mars, and Saturn in one's geniture – or birth chart – might tell an astrologically minded physician much about a patient's predisposition towards trouble of mind.

When in 1597 a twenty-year-old man called Robert Burton paid several visits to the astrological physician Simon Forman in London about a case of melancholy, Forman cast a horoscope each time as part of his medical notes since such information was considered vital to diagnosis.[2] The age is right, though we cannot be sure it was the same man who would later write *The Anatomy of Melancholy.* Whatever the case, Burton the author certainly paid attention to the influence of the stars. The varieties of melancholy depicted on the frontispiece to the *Anatomy* are each headed by corresponding astrological symbols, and Burton explains his fitness for the task of writing about melancholy by appealing to the planetary influences at his birth: 'Saturn was lord of my geniture, culminating, &c., and Mars principal significator of manners, in partile conjunction with my ascendant; both fortunate in their houses, etc.' (i.19). His memorial at Christ Church Cathedral in Oxford gives not only the date of his birth – 8 February 1577 – but also an astrological chart showing the time of day he was born, the precise coordinates of where he was born at the family home in Leicestershire, and the constellations that ruled over it.

The Devil's Bath

Melancholy was seen as a disease particularly susceptible to supernatural influences. The reasons for this are several: its many varieties; its interference with the proper workings of the imagination, which create the potential for sufferers to see and hear things that are not there; the influence of the heavens on the humours; and the black colour of the humour itself. A proverb of the time has it that 'a melancholy head is the devil's bath' ('caput melancholicum diaboli est balneum'). Burton explains that the colour of the humour makes for a useful disguise: 'the devil, spying his opportunity of such humours, drives them many times to despair, fury, rage, etc., mingling himself amongst those humours' (i.200).[3]

A Renaissance medical understanding of a case such as Katherine Gualter's, then, does not hinge on an either/or approach, where supernatural and physiological explanations are fundamentally separate. Instead, the causes are inextricably interwined. We see this in the case of a demoniac woman in Mantua whose symptoms included the ability to speak all languages, and whose physician treated her by purging her black bile. That this treatment was successful was not seen as proof that her condition had purely material causes, but rather that demonic possession worked through the vessel of the human body (i.200).

It was nonetheless a matter of some debate how far the devil could affect human beings, and the Christian tradition provides a whole spectrum of opinion on the subject. The devil was believed to have power on earth only through God's permission, and some argued that he could work upon the body but not upon the mind. Burton, however, was strongly of the opinion that he could affect both. If the devil can cause pestilential diseases such as murrain in cattle and crop failures, Burton argues, he can also hurt the bodies and minds of humans.

His example in support of this argument is a surprisingly familiar one: 'At Hammel in Saxony, *ann.* 1484. 20 *Junii* [20 June 1484], the devil, in likeness of a pied piper, carried away 130 children that were never after seen' (i.199).[4] The version of this story we know today from Robert Browning's poem has the children taken through a door in a mountainside into a paradisical land, glimpsed with longing by the child with the lame foot who does not quite make it there; the version that circulated in Burton's time was unequivocally sinister.

The devil meddles with human minds by worming his way into the humours and, through them, affecting the imagination. The children of Hamelin were not forced to follow the Pied Piper: they were charmed through the effects of his music on their minds. The Dutch physician Jason van de Velde (Pratensis, 1486–1555), author of a textbook on diseases of the brain, gives a highly literal explanation for how this works in practice: 'the devil, being a slender incomprehensible spirit, can easily insinuate and wind himself into human bodies, and, cunningly couched in our bowels, vitiate our healths, terrify our souls with fearful dreams, and shake our mind with furies' (i.200).

The devil's powers are channelled through a number of agents, and Burton's 'Digression of Spirits' gathers folklore and scholarship alike to demonstrate how spirits work and whether they can cause disease. Though his interest in the supernatural is clear, he doses it with a grain of scepticism: he dismisses as a 'foolish opinion' the idea that spirits are the ghosts of dead men, for instance (i.181). Just as the planets, elements, and bodily humours work in correspondence, so there are spirits to match: fiery devils live in volcanoes and tempt people towards precipices; aerial spirits start thunderstorms and whirlwinds, corrupt the air and cause plagues; water devils or nymphs disguise themselves as women and seduce men; and then there are terrestrial devils, 'fauns, satyrs, wood-nymphs, foliots, fairies, Robin Goodfellows, *trolli* [trolls], etc., which as they are most conversant with men, so do they do them most harm' (i.192; Figure 3.1). Though these last spirits can sometimes act benignly towards humans and help with household tasks, they also appear like ghosts, trick and frighten travellers into losing their way, or make their horses stumble.

Witches and magicians also fall into Burton's category of supernatural causes of melancholy. The trigger for the

FIGURE 3.1 *Robin Good-Fellow, His Mad Prankes and Merry Jests. Full of Honest Mirth, And Is a Fit Medicine For Melancholy* (1639).

young Katherine Gualter's experience was eating a cake that a woman had given her, and stories of derangement and possession caused by bewitchment – usually female – abound in Scandinavia and Germany. It is interesting to see Burton's argument in the light of other accounts of the period that claim witchcraft is caused *by* melancholy, rather than being a cause *of* it. In *The Discoverie of Witchcraft* (1584), Reginald Scot insists that the old women who claim magical powers are instead suffering from excesses of black bile:

> This melancholic humour (as the best physicians affirm) is the cause of all their strange, impossible, and incredible confessions: which are so fond, that I wonder how any man can be abused thereby. Howbeit, these affections, though they appear in the mind of man, yet are they bred in the body, and proceed from this humour, which is the very dregs of blood, nourishing and feeding those places, from whence proceed fears, cogitations, superstitions, fastings, labours, and such like.[5]

As women who have stopped menstruating, says Scot, they are especially prone to excesses of the humour, which gives them the illusion that they can fly, bring on a hailstorm, kill cattle, or curse their neighbour.

Scot supports his claim with the story of Ade Davie from the village of Selling in Kent, told to him by her husband Simon. Ade became suddenly afflicted with sadness, pensiveness, and trouble of mind, accompanied by insomnia and bouts of weeping. Her concerned husband tried to find out was wrong. Eventually she confessed that she had sold her soul to the devil and bewitched him and their children. Rather than accepting her word on this, Simon told her to be of good cheer since the bargain was void, and 'by the Grace of God, Jesus Christ shall unwitch us'. The next time that the devil came close, he prayed for her and had her read the psalms out loud.

At midnight, a great rumbling sound was heard below, which they thought was the devil trying to come upstairs but being prevented by the shield of their prayers. In fact, Scot adds, the sound came from a dog that had discovered a sheep's carcass and was noisily devouring it. He concludes that the evidence of her confession would have been enough for any court in the land to convict her of witchcraft, and she would have met a sorry end on the pyre. But 'God knoweth, she was innocent of any these crimes: howbeit she was brought low and pressed down with the weight of this humour, so as both her rest and sleep were taken away from her; & her fancies troubled and disquieted with despair.' Her husband's kindness and good sense saved her from the grim judgement that other women met, and she fully recovered from her melancholic condition.[6]

Although Scot claims that his medical contemporaries dismiss witchcraft as natural and physiological in origin, there was no firm consensus on this point in Renaissance England. Burton lists authorities on both sides of the debate – physicians, philosophers, and theologians – and certainly seems to believe in stories of witchcraft himself. Witches can 'cure and cause most diseases to such as they love or hate, and this of melancholy amongst the rest' (i.205). Nonetheless, Burton stresses that their spells and charms have no power in themselves but rather are the means that the devil uses to delude people.

A great gatherer of opinions, stories, and views about melancholy, Burton is hardly consistent – and perhaps has little interest in being so. Later on in the *Anatomy*, he begins the 'Immediate Cause of these precedent Symptoms' with some reassuring words:

> To give some satisfaction to melancholy men that are troubled with these symptoms, a better means in my judgment cannot be taken than to show them the causes whence they proceed; not from devils as they suppose, or that they are bewitched or forsaken of God, hear or see, etc., as many of them think, but from natural and inward causes; that so knowing them, they may better avoid the effects, or at least endure them with more patience. (i.419)

Perhaps Burton would not see this as inconsistency at all, but instead as a way of modifying his rhetoric to suit the therapeutic context. That the devil exists and takes advantage of the melancholy humour, he is certain. To a melancholic, however, self-accusation may only cause further damage, and those who think they are possessed or bewitched may be experiencing the results of 'gross fumes, ascending from black humours' (i.419) to affect their brains. That is what happened to Ade Davie, after all.

Love Magic

Though supernatural forces were believed to have damaging effects on the human body and mind, not all cases were treated with the same level of seriousness. As we will see in more depth in Chapters 5 and 6, Burton devotes separate sections of *The Anatomy of Melancholy* to exploring two distinct categories of the disease: love melancholy and religious melancholy. In the first, Burton gives himself leave to 'refresh my Muse a little, and my weary readers, to expatiate in this delightsome field ... to season a surly discourse with a more pleasing aspersion of love matters' (iii.6). To fall in love can be a melancholic disorder, and – as he argues – it is not necessarily the result of human attraction.

Though charms, potions, amulets, and spells are for Burton 'unlawful means' (iii.129) to provoke love, they are also the stuff of comedy. In *A Midsummer Night's Dream* – famously – that terrestrial spirit or Robin Goodfellow, Puck, uses a love potion to anoint the eyes of Lysander and Demetrius while they sleep. But even such a plot device seems relatively conventional by comparison to some of the examples Burton gives of people who have been magically allured into love, not least the story of Emperor Charlemagne, taken from Petrarch:

He foolishly doted upon a woman of mean favour and condition, many years together, wholly delighting in her company, to the great grief and indignation of his friends and followers. When she was dead, he did embrace her corpse, as Apollo did the bay-tree for his Daphne, and caused her coffin (richly embalmed and decked with jewels) to be carried about with him, over which he still lamented. At last a venerable bishop that followed his court, prayed earnestly to God (commiserating his lord and master's case) to know the true cause of this mad passion, and whence it proceeded; it was revealed to him, in fine, that the cause of the emperor's mad love lay under the dead woman's tongue. The bishop went hastily to the carcass, and took a small ring thence; upon the removal the emperor abhorred the corpse, and, instead of it, fell as furiously in love with the bishop, he would not suffer him to be out of his presence; which when the bishop perceived, he flung the ring into the midst of a great lake, where the king then was. From that hour the emperor neglected all his other houses, dwelt at Ache [Aachen], built a fair house in the midst of the marsh, to his infinite expense, and a temple by it, where after he was buried, and in which city all his posterity ever since use to be crowned. (iii.131)[7]

Stories of 'mad love' induced by occult means have in common the idea of transgression, which the legend of Charlemagne fulfils on multiple fronts. The victim is tricked or charmed into loving someone too young or too old, or of the wrong social class, or of the same sex, or a different race, or not human – or not even alive. And, as is the case for Charlemagne, this magic makes the victim behave in undecorous and often embarrassing ways.

That Burton sees a story such as this as an example of melancholy is linked to his view of the human will. When a person becomes melancholic, her ability to choose becomes compromised by the strength of her emotions, so that she is unable to make free, rational decisions. The imagination or 'fancy' holds sway over the body and mind, and it is vulnerable to being deceived by external agents (see Figure 3.2). Burton classes magical potions as forms of 'Artificial Allurements', in the same category as bawds and panders who trick young men and maidens into assignations, supply aphrodisiacs to enhance sexual performance, and corrupt nuns and monks through nefarious means. Magic takes away choice and charms the victim into doing what the perpetrator wants.

Though Burton has no doubt of the power of physical beauty, he records examples from history where there may have been more than meets the eye: Plutarch records, for example, that 'Cleopatra used philters [potions] to inveigle Antony, amongst other allurements' (iii.130). Love is a form of tyranny, he says (quoting Xenophon), 'worse than any disease, and they that are troubled with it desire to be free and cannot, but are harder bound than if they were in iron chains' (iii.161). And since love enslaves people and holds them captive, it is much like the other types of melancholy which trap sufferers.

It may be that love magic does not work on a supernatural level at all, but that what it achieves is 'merely effected by natural causes, as by man's blood chemically prepared' (iii.131–2). The substances stimulate changes in the body's temperament, causing love through humoral imbalance. Well-known love philtres mentioned by ancient authors include mandrake roots, aubergines, gem stones, a particular hair in the tail of a wolf, a swallow's heart, a viper's tongue, a piece of rope that has been used to hang a man, and the penis of a horse. Burton does not give the full details of what you should do with these things in order to make someone fall in love with you; perhaps it is too dangerous to explain (and some of them he even lists in Latin, concealing them from those readers who can only read English). He has no doubt that they are effective, though their supposedly magical properties may have a more rational explanation.

One last example that Burton finds of these powers in action is at 'that hot bath at Aix in Germany, wherein Cupid once dipped his arrows, which ever since hath a peculiar virtue to make them lovers all that wash in it' (iii.132). These are the spa waters at Aachen, and Burton typically has it both ways: the medical writers who claim that there are natural explanations for this phenomenon may be quite correct, but that is no reason to drop the myth that it was Cupid's arrows which gave the water its powerful property. Though he does not make the connection, it was at Aachen – 'Ache', 'Aix' – where Charlemagne lived out his final days. The marsh and lake from Petrarch's tale were thermal springs, and it is far more probable that Charlemagne built his palace around them because the mineral water was therapeutic for his ailments than because a magic ring had been flung into them. But why let that get in the way of a good story?

Religious Melancholy

Minerals and drugs can have powerful effects on both bodies and minds but – even if there is a natural explanation – the devil may be behind them. If someone falls madly in love with the wrong person, or behaves strangely without seeming to be able to control it, supernatural forces may be the source of their melancholic complaint, working through the immediate causes which are simply natural ones. Then again – and this is melancholy's two-sided coin – the sufferer may be deceived into thinking that his or her illness is demonic in origin when it is anything but.

This dilemma of discernment is at work in another variety of Renaissance melancholy, and one particular to Burton's approach: that brought on by religious experience. Burton is unique in classifying 'Religious Melancholy' as its own category, a subdivision of love melancholy. It was a term he introduced and which went on to have a significant influence on writers right through to the nineteenth century, not just in Britain but also in America.[8]

Who are religious melancholics? They are people who prophesy the date of the end of the world to the nearest day; ascetics who submit themselves to punishing regimes of fasting, self-flagellation, and sleepless nights; hermits who live in caves or anchorites walled up in tiny cells; visionaries who dream of direct revelations from God; schismatics who claim to know how many people God has saved or damned (and usually give a higher number for the latter than the former). They may be dangerous not only to themselves but also to others. They believe that their faith is so strong that they are impervious to disease and will go into infected houses during an epidemic. Or they spread infection by a different route, travelling the country and preaching heresy among the people:

> It will run along like murrain in cattle, scab in sheep ... as he that is bitten with a mad dog bites others, and all in the end become mad; either out of affection of novelty, simplicity, blind zeal, hope and fear, the giddy-headed multitude will embrace it, and without farther examination approve it. (iii.366)

Religious melancholics are driven by the tenacity of their beliefs into a fervent zeal to convert others and some of Burton's most excoriating words in the *Anatomy* are saved for them. His attack on them is strongly inflected by the animosity that was typical of early Stuart religious conformists towards, on the one hand, 'superstitious' Roman Catholics and, on the other, 'zealous' puritan non-conformists.

Burton uses the twin weapons of medicine and theology to denounce extremes of religious behaviour: extremes by implicit contrast, of course, to the carefully positioned moderation of his own Church. Devout practices such as fasting, contemplation, and solitude, when taken to excess, become 'certain rams by which the devil doth batter and work upon the strongest constitutions' (iii.342). Again we see a mixture of supernatural influences and natural causes being ascribed to these melancholic cases: a spare or poor diet, lack of sleep, and being alone too much are means to disrupt the body's normal temperature, of which the devil takes advantage as a way to corrupt the bodies and souls of the pious.

This is how he interprets the recent cases of three Englishmen who behaved in fanatical ways. There was Peter Burchett, a puritan and lawyer who in 1573 attempted to murder Queen Elizabeth I's favourite courtier Sir Christopher Hatton, but got the wrong man and stabbed the naval commander Sir John Hawkins instead; he was suspected of mental instability, but still hanged. There was Matthew Hamont, a ploughwright from Norfolk who declared that Christ was not God, and was burned at the stake for heresy in Norwich in 1579. And then there was William Hacket, the maltster-turned-prophet from Northamptonshire who declared that he was the Messiah and who became convinced that he was immortal, proving this by wrestling with the lions in the Tower of London and surviving unscathed. He and his disciples prophesied that he would take over the throne from Elizabeth, and despite a defence plea that he was insane, he was found guilty of treason and hanged, drawn, and quartered at Cheapside in 1591 (iii.371).[9]

His examples are not confined to England. Though Burton's treatment of religious melancholy as its own category was innovative, he found cases documented in the textbooks of a number of continental medical writers. One such was Ercole Sassonia (Hercules de Saxonia, 1551–1607), who taught at one of the great European centres of medicine, Padua, and who provides the last tale of supernatural melancholy in this chapter. As Burton retells it, Sassonia had 'a prophet committed to his charge in Venice, that thought he was Elias [Elijah]'. Since Elijah fasted for forty days and forty nights as he went up Mount Horeb to speak with God (1 Kings 19:8), the self-professed prophet decided to do the same. He refused all food and started to waste away. Sassonia treated both the delusion and the symptom by the same curious method, using the Bible as his aid. As the Old Testament account tells it, before Elijah undertook his long fast and journey, he was sleeping in the wilderness when on two occasions an angel appeared, woke him up and told him to 'arise and eat', providing him with the sustenance he needed (1 Kings 19:5–8). So Sassonia did the same: 'he dressed a fellow in angel's attire, that said he came from heaven to bring him divine food, and by that means stayed his fast, administered his physic; so by the mediation of this forged angel he was cured' (iii.378). The scriptural narrative provided a prompt which shook the man out of his fixed belief; by eating, as Elijah did, he broke the fast that maintained the delusion. This kind of 'playing along' as a means of treating a delusion is a common one in the Renaissance; to which we will return in the next chapter.

There are times when Burton sounds a note of sympathy for the people he deems to be religious melancholics, though that sympathy is certainly limited. Medical responses are often the best, he counsels: 'We have frequently such prophets and dreamers amongst us, whom we persecute with fire and faggot; I think the most compendious cure, for some of them at least, had been in Bedlam' (iii.378–9). Cases like Burchett's, Hamont's, and Hacket's show that those who were suspected to be of unsound mind did not necessarily escape the full and violent force of the law. By proposing the idea that they might be suffering from melancholy or insanity, Burton suggests that their will is not their own and that they are better treated than punished – though confinement in Bedlam would hardly be likely to make them better.

The bodily humour black bile was a breeding ground for supernatural influences, or for symptoms so strange that they masqueraded as the supernatural. Their effects could be disconcerting and unsettling – as they were in the case of Katherine Gualter – and even though doubt was cast at times on the authenticity of what looked like demonic possession or magical powers, writers such as Robert Burton took seriously the idea that not all melancholy was of this world. As we have seen, the relationship between genuinely supernatural or spiritual influences and the natural effects of the body could not easily be separated, and it was a hard task for healers – medical practitioners and clergy alike – to discern wisely how best to treat such cases of melancholy. The disease's porous borders encompassed not only witchcraft and possession but magically induced love, religious zealotry, and superstition: all places where mental distress and delusion might ferment. In the next chapter, we shall see how unshakeable beliefs form an integral part of melancholic experience, by looking at cases of patients who, like the Venetian would-be prophet, were consumed by delusional ideas, and at the approaches of those physicians who treated them.

PART 2
SYMPTOMS

FIGURE 4.1 A hooded physician examining a urine specimen, brought to him by an elderly woman. Woodcut by Jost Amman (1568).

4
Delusions

The pleasantest dotage that ever I read was of one *Sienois* a gentleman, who had resolved with himself not to piss, but to die rather, and that because he imagined that when he first pissed, all his town would be drowned. The physicians showing him that all his body, and ten thousand more such as his, were not able to contain so much as might drown the least house in the town, could not change his mind from this foolish imagination. In the end they seeing his obstinacy, and in what danger he put his life, found out a pleasant invention. They caused the next house to be set on fire, & all the bells in the town to ring, they persuaded diverse servants to cry, to the fire, to the fire, & therewithall send of those of the best account in the town to crave help, and show the gentleman that there is but one way to save the town, and that it was, that he should piss quickly and quench the fire. Then this silly melancholic man which abstained from pissing for fear of losing his town, taking it for granted, that it was now in great hazard, pissed and emptied his bladder of all that was in it, and was himself by that means preserved.[1]

The story of the gentleman from Siena in Italy who was unable to urinate is one of the stranger cases recorded in Renaissance medical literature, and certainly has one of the most outlandish and inventive therapies. It is found in the writings of André du Laurens, who was not only physician to King Henri IV of France but also – like Robert Burton, who repeated the story – a great documenter of melancholy. His *Discours des maladies mélancoliques* (1594, translated into English in 1599) contains a much-quoted collection of the 'Histories of certain melancholic persons', all of whom have delusions.

The story bears the hallmarks of melancholy's diseased imagination. First of all, the gentleman develops an unshakeable belief which governs his behaviour. He cannot urinate (it should be said that 'piss' did not have any coarse overtones in the period) because, if he allows himself to, he believes that he will drown his whole town. Then his physicians try logical persuasion but it does not work: no amount of labour will convince their patient that the cubic capacity of his bladder is not up to the job. So they decide on a quite different course of action: instead of fighting against the delusion, they will work with it.

Entering the reality of the melancholy man's mind, the physicians design a therapy that makes sense from his perspective, if not their own. They do not do this by halves. Rather than simply pretending that there is a fire, such is their commitment to authenticity that they start a real one, no doubt since the patient must smell real smoke in order to be convinced. Indeed, their efforts resemble a grand theatrical spectacle: they trigger the town's fire alarm system by ringing the church bells; they give servants bit parts with lines to shout out; they make the civic worthies join in the persuasion. They turn the patient's delusion into a cause for heroism. The final feature of this story is a common one in cases of delusion: once they find the right therapy, the treatment works instantly. In Burton's retelling of the story, 'he made water, and was immediately cured' (ii.114–15).

A Renaissance melancholic's delusion is tenacious but ultimately fragile. It is like that source of fascination for scientists in the later seventeenth century, the

Prince Rupert's drop: a tear-shaped piece of glass made by dripping molten glass into cold water. When cooled, the drop has immense tensile strength and the bulb end can withstand any number of blows from a hammer. But snap the tail end with your fingers or squeeze it with pliers and the whole drop will shatter into a thousand pieces.[2] Likewise, Renaissance physicians try to find the sweet spot where a melancholic delusion will disintegrate. Often that involves seeing the patient's experience from within, as well as addressing the bodily complaint. If the patient can be cajoled or tricked into urinating when he has vowed not to, or eating when she has refused all food, that simple action may unlock the cure. The underlying reasons why a patient might develop a particular delusion or phobia are rarely addressed in Renaissance medical texts – at least, not in the ways we might expect.

This chapter explores the wide variety of melancholic delusions that are charted in Renaissance medical writing. Physicians gathered these stories into collections and recycled them from one textbook to the next, as much for their curiosity value as for what they had to teach about the human mind. That much is evident in the way that André du Laurens introduces the Sienese gentleman's story as the 'pleasantest dotage' (mental impairment or weakness). Writers on melancholy certainly had an eye for the unusual and exotic, but retailing these cases was not done simply to ridicule. The Sienese patient is described as a 'silly melancholic', but 'silly' in the sixteenth and seventeenth centuries had the primary meaning of unfortunate, wretched, weak and vulnerable rather than foolish and ridiculous. In the original French, Du Laurens calls him 'ce pauvre melancholique': 'this poor melancholic'.[3]

The word hints at more compassion than we might first give the writer credit for.

Although we are using the word 'delusion' to describe a particular set of experiences, Renaissance writers had no single word to label them. They were recognised as a symptom of melancholy rather than as a disorder or syndrome in their own right, as they are in psychology today. The word 'delusion' was certainly current in the sixteenth and seventeenth centuries but Burton never uses it; instead, he describes such an experience as a 'conceit' (that is, 'something conceived in the mind'; 'a fanciful notion'), a 'chimera', a 'humour', or by the Latin word 'praestigium' (which means 'delusion' or 'illusion').[4] Renaissance physicians made no attempt to categorise these experiences by type, but – as we will see – there are clusters of similar stories which display a common set of associations concerning the body and mind and their functions, and the desires and fears of sufferers. These have much to tell us not only about the way Renaissance melancholy works, but also about the preoccupations of a whole culture.

Delusions of the Body

The Sienese gentleman who feared urinating suffered from a fixation that was strongly corporeal in nature. The stopping of healthy flow of the humours was seen to be a cause of illness, so it would not be surprising to a Renaissance physician to find that refusing to urinate might be linked to significant mental disturbance. Anything that prevented flow might have consequences for the mind as well as the body, and this was demonstrated in injuries too: the Portuguese physician João Rodrigues de Castelo Branco (Amatus Lusitanus, 1511–68) records a fascinating instance of a man with a boil in his arm who, after it healed, went mad, but when the wound was reopened, was cured of his madness (i.379).

Letting your bladder over-fill itself and neglecting to empty it was in itself a disease of scholars – who were more prone than most people to melancholy. After the great classical scholar Isaac Casaubon (1559–1614) died, a postmortem revealed that his bladder was malformed and that the supplementary bladder was nearly six times as large as the main chamber. This was partly down to a congenital disorder, and partly because Casaubon had been in the habit of ignoring the calls of nature while he was over-absorbed in his work (a condition now known as Nurses' Bladder).[5]

The Sienese patient's disorder thus mirrored a condition with natural origins, but in this case it took on an added layer of disproportion. It was not that he had simply neglected the call of nature, but that he became incapable of heeding it. His will was overthrown to the extent that he lost the mental ability to perform a basic bodily function. Paradoxically, this happened by his mind going into a kind of hyper-control. Du Laurens' account speaks of his 'obstinacy': what has broken down is his reason, now under the sway of a diseased imagination. This is mind over matter indeed.

By far the majority of reported cases of melancholic delusion in Renaissance medicine centre on patients' false beliefs about their own bodies. The stories repeated from one medical textbook to the next tell of patients with sensory distortions, or who believed that part or all of their body was in disproportion to the world around it, or who were convinced that their flesh was of a different substance. One melancholic thought that he had no head, until his physician put a heavy iron hat on him and forced him to admit that his head hurt. Another, a young scholar, believed he had an enormous nose and was afraid of moving his head around; he was cured by his doctor's pretending to cut it off and showing him a large piece of flesh he had removed. And several cases tell of people who believed that they had missing limbs, even though they could see them: one such person was Artemidorus the grammarian, who saw a crocodile and was so terrified of it that he became convinced it had eaten his arm and leg.[6]

Another common belief among melancholics centres on the idea that their body has been occupied by another living being. Reptiles and amphibians are a speciality: Burton describes the case of a man suffering from hypochondriacal or 'windy melancholy' who 'by reason of those ascending vapours and gripings rumbling beneath, will not be persuaded but that he hath a serpent in his guts, a viper' (i.412); another of a woman who believed she had swallowed an eel or a snake. We saw in Chapter 3 the story of Katherine Gualter, who voided a live eel while being seemingly under the curse of witchcraft. But not every patient believed that the devil was at the heart of their disorder.

The case of the man with a viper in his guts stems from the patient's misperception of what his senses told him was going on inside himself. We might see this as characteristic of a Renaissance medical system that taught people to attend to the way their bodies felt, and relate those feelings in quite direct ways to inner processes. Michael Schoenfeldt has observed that it is easy for us 'to underestimate both the seductive coherence of Galenic humoral theory and its experiential suppleness'. Yet, 'when one gets over the initial unfamiliarity of a particular description of a bodily process, one is struck by the fact that this is indeed how bodies feel as if they are behaving'. For instance, whereas we might describe a burning sensation in the stomach and attribute it to indigestion or an ulcer, a person in the sixteenth or seventeenth century experiencing the same symptom might relate it to a literal burning: overheating of the stomach, an excess of the hot, dry humour choler, or a humour becoming adust (burnt up, corrupted). Galenic medicine may not describe the body as we now know that it functions, but it does a remarkable job of describing the body as we experience it.[7] So the conclusion that the melancholy man reached about his uncomfortable gaseous rumblings is, in some ways, a literal-minded extension of Galenic ways of thinking: a feeling *like* there is something moving within his stomach and a rumbling sound *like* an animal became a feeling and sound *of* it, living within him.

Whereas his delusion about a viper in his guts is based on pre-existing symptoms within his body, other delusions of a similar kind come from something taken into the body. Burton records a case from the Swiss physician Felix Platter:

> a countryman of his … by chance falling into a pit where frogs and frogs' spawn was, and a little of that water swallowed, began to suspect that he had likewise swallowed frogs' spawn, and with that conceit and fear, his phantasy [imagination]

wrought so far, that he verily thought he had young live frogs in his belly, *qui vivebant ex alimento suo*, that lived by his nourishment, and was so certainly persuaded of it, that for many years following he could not be rectified in his conceit. (i.412)

His delusion developed out of fear, and (as we saw in Chapter 1) this is one of the defining features of melancholy and is the source of both sudden and long-term effects. The patient's anxiety was no passing whim; his case is remarkable both for its longevity and for the extreme action it caused him to take:

He studied physic seven years together to cure himself, travelled into Italy, France and Germany to confer with the best physicians about it, and *anno* 1609, asked his [Felix Platter's] counsel amongst the rest; he told him it was wind, his conceit, etc. but … no saying would serve, it was no wind, but real frogs: "and do you not hear them croak?" Platerus would have deceived him by putting live frogs into his excrements; but he, being a physician himself, would not be deceived. (i.412–13)

To embark on a programme of medical education as self-therapy for a delusion is certainly unusual, although the man's course of action might resonate with those people who live with chronic illness or disability and become experts in their own condition. The irony is that the patient educated himself out of a cure: unlike the Sienese gentleman, this Swiss man was not fooled by the pious fraud that Platter attempted on him. Despite his strange belief, he was a 'wise and learned man otherwise'; one of the common features of melancholy delusion is that in every other respect, the person's behaviour is perfectly conventional. Though many patients are tricked into an instant cure, this man's recovery took much longer.

Eventually, it was his persistence over seven years which cured him rather than any conjuring tricks – and which left him as a qualified doctor.

Part of the Swiss man's delusion rested upon sensory experience; he could hear the frogs croaking within him and believed that other people would too. Hearing things such as music, bells, animals, or voices is a widely reported symptom in Renaissance casebooks, as are other forms of sensory delusion. King Louis XI of France (1423–83) was said to have descended into a state of severe melancholy where, among many other symptoms, he was convinced that his body and everything around him stank. Though his attendants burned strong-smelling perfumes in his chambers, it made little difference to him. He became unable to eat, claiming that 'he felt a foul stinking savour ascending up out of his body up into his brain', and died still labouring under the delusion.[8] Though his delusion sounds similar to what is now known in psychiatric terminology as olfactory reference syndrome – the false belief that your body smells offensive to others – Louis XI's condition has a Galenic inflection: he imagined the smell as emanating from the humours within him and producing foul vapours that affected his thoughts.

Several olfactory delusions recorded in Renaissance writing have a link to a pre-existing illness. André du Lauren's collection of case histories includes one of a renowned French poet who fell sick with fever, which was accompanied with bouts of insomnia. To help him sleep, his doctors prescribed him an ointment called populeon (made from the buds of the black poplar) which was rubbed on his temples and nose. Though he recovered from the fever, from that time onwards he developed a wild aversion to the smell of populeon. He not only avoided it himself but 'all that came near him he imagined to scent of it, and would let no man talk with him but aloof off, or wear any new clothes, because he thought still they smelled of it; in all other things wise and discreet, he would talk sensibly, save only in this' (i.403).[9] The delusion started with the trauma of a dangerous illness, but for Renaissance physicians it also started with a typically melancholy-inducing occasion: the sweats of a fever took heat and moisture away from the patient's body, thereby increasing black bile.

The Glass Delusion

Melancholy delusions are as interesting for the behaviour they prompt as for the 'conceit' itself. For the French poet, for instance, his disproportionate fear of populeon ointment caused him to 'let no man talk with him but aloof off'. It might seem understandable that a person who has had a dangerous fever would develop a fear of others coming too close, either because he himself has been feared as a carrier of contagious disease or because he is frightened of catching something else. The man's aversion to a strong ointment carries a memory of the sickbed into the everyday, where he lived out an enforced social distancing.

When Renaissance physicians studied symptoms such as these, they often turned to the structures of Islamic medicine to guide them. The Persian philosopher and medical writer Muhammad ibn Zakariya' al-Razi (Rhazes, 854–925) divides symptoms into three degrees. The first is false thinking: misconstruing and distorting things, 'aggravating every thing they conceive or fear'.

The second is false thinking as it comes through in speech and sound: talking to oneself or in gibberish; articulating the thoughts as if they are true; crying or laughing. The third degree is putting this false thinking into practice, living out the thoughts and speech through actions. So the French poet's delusion emerges in the second degree as he tells others to keep away from him, and in the third degree as he physically steps away from them.[10]

We can see these different degrees of symptomatic behaviour at work in perhaps the most famous melancholy delusion of all: the belief that one is made from glass. Like the olfactory delusion, this one induces a fear of others coming too near, in this case because the sufferer is terrified of being shattered into pieces. Cases recorded in the Middle Ages and Renaissance include patients who believe that they are made entirely of glass, or that they have a glass bottom and cannot sit down, or that they are made of a specific object such as a urine flask – an item which was a typical symbol of the physician (Figure 4.1) – or an oil lamp, or that their chest is made of glass and others can see straight into them. Perhaps the most famous sufferer was King Charles VI of France (1386–1422), who among many signs of mental instability believed that his body was made of glass and refused to let anyone come near him or touch him; he had specially reinforced clothing made to support his body so that it did not crack.[11]

André du Laurens records one such case from his own time, of

> a great Lord, which thought himself to be glass, and had not his imagination troubled, otherwise than in this one only thing, for he could speak marvellously well of any other thing:

he used commonly to sit, and took great delight that his friends should come and see him, but so as that he would desire them, that they would not come near unto him.[12]

Once again, the delusion manifests itself in keeping others at a distance. It is striking that, as with Louis XI and Charles VI, this case involves someone who is socially elevated. We might conjecture that their cases are connected to a desire to keep others safely out of immediate range, perhaps through fear of an assassination attempt or indeed of contagious disease. But it is equally striking that Renaissance writers on melancholy do not explore the possible reasons why these patients are so averse to social contact. The approaches of modern-day psychiatry towards such a disorder (and the glass delusion has been reported in modern contexts) are quite alien to the ways a Renaissance physician would consider it.[13] From the perspective of André du Laurens, the most important feature of the great lord's *noli me tangere* is what it tells us about the astonishing degree to which human reason can be affected by the imagination (see Figure 4.2). A man can be perfectly rational in every other way except for being troubled 'in this one only thing'.

Of all the delusions recorded in the Middle Ages and Renaissance, the glass delusion is the one that most captured the popular imagination and found its way into a rich variety of literary forms. Miguel de Cervantes' 'Doctor Glass-Case' ('El licenciado vidriera', 1613) is a short story about a man who, like the melancholy French poet, develops a delusion as a result of sickness. Tomás Rodaja is a well-travelled and highly educated young man who has risen out of poverty to become a Doctor of Laws at the University of Salamanca. A woman who has fallen in love with him gives him a quince laced with a love philtre, in an attempt to have him requite her feelings. The charm does not work: instead he is poisoned and confined to a sickbed for six months.

Even as he recovers from his bodily illness, he starts to become convinced that he is made entirely of glass. He shouts at anyone who tries to come near him, has a wooden case built that is filled with soft cotton to save him from shattering, and enacts all kinds of self-protective measures:

> In passing through the streets, Rodaja was in the habit of walking carefully in the middle of them, lest a tile should fall from the houses upon his head and break it. In the summer he slept in the open air, and in the winter he lodged at one of the inns, where he buried himself in straw to his throat, remarking that this was the most proper and secure bed for men of glass. When it thundered, Rodaja trembled like an aspen leaf, and would rush out into the fields, not returning to the city until the storm had passed.[14]

The delusion persists for a full two years until he is cured by a monk (we do not learn by what means). But throughout this time he becomes renowned not just for his strange behaviour but also for his wisdom. While – inevitably – boys throw stones at him to see if he really will break, other people approach him to ask for advice on their personal dilemmas. His pronouncements reveal him to be a philosopher, a political and social commentator, a lover of good poetry, and a witty satirist. The delusion sets him apart from the normal social order and in so doing, enables him to observe its follies – rather like Democritus, the laughing philosopher.

Explaining Delusions

What is it about glass in particular that makes melancholics prone to this delusion? Though the case histories and stories point to the fact that glass is a fragile and transparent substance, Renaissance medical theorists do not make a direct connection between those properties and the mental state of the sufferer. In other words, they do not suggest that a person such as Du Laurens' great lord or Tomás Rodaja believes he is made of glass because he feels mentally fragile or feels exposed to the gaze of others. Instead, one of the ways they explain delusion is as a profound correspondence between an external substance and the disposition of the person's body. Du Laurens argues that 'such as of an extreme dry temperature, and have the brain also very dry; if they happen commonly to look upon some pitcher or glass (which are things very usual and common) they will judge themselves to be pitchers or glasses': it is black bile's characteristic dryness which, coupled with sensory suggestion, creates this false belief in the mind of someone with an excess of melancholy.[15]

An ingenious enactment both of this delusion and of its cause can be found in an unlikely source: an English academic play of the early seventeenth century. Thomas Tomkis' *Lingua* (1607) is an allegorical drama in which the five senses compete with one another in order to prove who is the best and win the crown and robes that Lingua (speech) offers as prizes. Tactus (touch) steals the prizes and sits on top of them to hide them from Olfactus (smell), pretending that he has a glass delusion so that

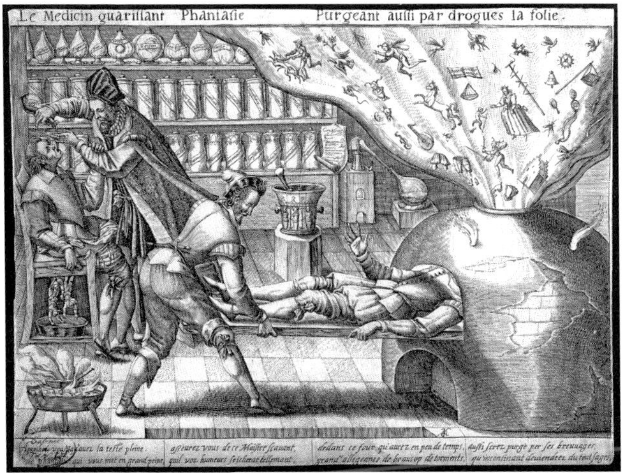

FIGURE 4.2 *A Surgery Where All Fantasy and Follies Are Purged and Good Qualities Are Prescribed.* Line engraving by M. Greuter (c. 1600).

Olfactus will not come too close. He enacts this deception rather convincingly:

No sooner had I parted out of doors,
But up I held my hands before my face:
To shield mine eyes from th' light's piercing beams,
When I protest I saw the sun as clear
Through these my palms as through a prospective
[perspective glass]:
No marvel, for when I beheld my fingers,
I saw my fingers near transform'd to glass.

When Tactus sits down, he 'discovers' that he is not just glass, but he is a urinal (that is, a glass urine flask) – a comical anti-climax after we have heard the beautiful account of his seeing the sun's light shining through his hands.

Olfactus is horrified and tries to cure him by explaining how it has come about:

See the strange working of dull melancholy,
Whose drossy drying the feeble brain
Corrupts the sense, deludes the intellect.
And in the soul's fair table falsely graves [engraves]
Whole squadrons of fantastical chimeras
And thousand vain imaginations:
Making some think their heads as big as horses,
Some that th'are dead, some that th'are turned to wolves:
As now it makes him think himself all glass,
Tactus dissuade thyself, thou doest but think so.[16]

Faced with Tactus' strange imaginings, Olfactus is sure that the root of the problem is in his black bile, the fumes of which corrupt the brain; it is melancholy's quality of dryness that causes these 'chimeras'. The examples he gives are all taken straight from textbooks such as Du Laurens' *Discourse … of Melancholike Diseases* (1599) and clearly he is well versed in medical writing, even though his attempts to cure Tactus are rather limp. Of course, Tactus is faking his delusion anyway, which is fully exploited for its farcical potential in such subtle lines as 'I am an urinal; I dare not stir / For fear of cracking in the bottom.'

While humoral theory provides the framework for explaining mental disturbances – as we see at work in the play – nonetheless Renaissance medical writers do not treat the imagination as working entirely at random in the false beliefs it generates in individuals. They also link these beliefs to the way of life these patients lead. For Du Laurens and his contemporaries, black bile 'will imprint in melancholic men the objects most answerable to their condition of life and ordinary actions'.[17] A clear example might be found in glass: it was an expensive product, and so its prevalence in the mental disorders of the well born is, in part, an outcome of the fact that this luxury substance surrounded them in their windows, their tableware, and the flasks used by the physicians they could afford to consult. Elsewhere in the *Anatomy*, Robert Burton tells the story of 'Cotys, king of Thrace, that brake a company of fine glasses presented to him, with his own hands, lest he should be overmuch moved when they were broken by chance' (ii.203). Glass's beauty and preciousness are linked to its delicacy, providing a reflective surface on which the wealthy might perceive their own states. A poorer person might imagine that they were an earthenware jug: still breakable, but more humble and functional.

Though most of the delusions we have seen belong to elite patients – French kings, a nobleman – there are a few stories attached to people of lower social class. Burton records the case of a baker in Ferrara, Italy who 'thought he was composed of butter, and durst not sit in the sun or come near the fire for fear of being melted' (i.403). Here is a classic case of a melancholic whose symptoms are linked to what Du Laurens calls his 'disposition of life'. Rather than avoiding other people for fear he would break, the baker's fear was that his body would lose its form and melt away if he came near the tools of his trade: the fire he used to bake his bread. His mental disturbance thus prevented him from carrying out his job – a delusion with very severe consequences for his livelihood.

And several delusions centre on social status itself. Delusions of grandeur, to use a modern phrase, became well known in the nineteenth century. Laure Murat has shown that, in the year when Napoleon's remains were repatriated to France, 1840, a Paris asylum admitted fourteen men who all claimed to be Napoleon.[18] Yet, a similar delusion is found in Renaissance medical literature. Robert Burton ascribes this to a person's pre-existing character:

> If an ambitious man become melancholy, he forthwith thinks he is a king, an emperor, a monarch, and walks alone, pleasing himself with a vain hope of some future preferment, or present as he supposeth, and with all acts a Lord's part, takes upon him to be some statesman or magnifico, makes congees [bows], gives entertainment, looks big, etc. Francisco Sansovino records of a melancholy man in Cremona, that would not be induced to believe but that he was Pope, gave pardons, made cardinals, etc. (i.404)

Though these delusions normally belong to men, Burton also records the case of a gentlewoman in Mantua who believed that she was married to a king and 'if she had found by chance a piece of glass in a muck-hill or in the street, she would say that it was a jewel sent from her lord and husband' (i.404). The melancholics afflicted by these delusions are especially prone to enacting ceremonies, finding everyday items to use as props, and elaborately performing their assumed roles as wielders of power and prestige.

Imagining Delusions

We have seen the central role that imagination plays in generating delusions or 'conceits', and, in turn, the inspiration that the glass delusion in particular has given to drama and fiction. Renaissance case histories of melancholics living out delusional fantasies may have had a wider, albeit less overt influence on imaginative literature. Perhaps stories about delusions of social status, for instance, were creative prompts to Shakespeare, whose early play *The Taming of the Shrew* begins with a group of young gentlemen tricking the dead-drunk tinker Christopher Sly all too easily into believing that he is himself a lord, and that his former life is a dream; when they put on a play for him (*The Taming of the Shrew* itself), it is for medicinal reasons, 'Seeing too much sadness hath congealed your blood –/ And melancholy is the nurse of frenzy'.[19]

The disrupted and disruptive lives of delusional melancholics extend beyond the medical textbooks where they are recorded, and they even extend beyond the sixteenth and seventeenth centuries. Among the eighteenth-century readers of *The Anatomy of Melancholy* was Jonathan Swift. In *Gulliver's Travels* (1719), the protagonist's experiences on the islands of Lilliput and Brobdingnag hold up a fictional mirror to those earlier tales of melancholics suffering from delusions of disproportion recorded by Burton: 'one thinks himself a giant, another a dwarf', 'another thinks himself so little, that he can creep into a mouse-hole' (i.403).[20] And one story of a Renaissance delusion finds a particular echo.

While he is on the tiny island of Lilliput, the (relative) giant Gulliver is called upon in an emergency. Awaking at midnight to the sound of cries for help, he discovers that the Lilliputian empress' apartments in the royal palace are on fire. The citizens' thimble-sized buckets of water fail to quench the flames and the palace seems doomed to burn to the ground, until Gulliver thinks of an unlikely expedient:

I had, the evening before, drunk plentifully of a most delicious wine called *glimigrim*, (the Blefuscudians call it *flunec*, but ours is esteemed the better sort,) which is very diuretic. By the luckiest chance in the world, I had not discharged myself of any part of it. The heat I had contracted by coming very near the flames, and by labouring to quench them, made the wine begin to operate by urine; which I voided in such a quantity, and applied so well to the proper places, that in three minutes the fire was wholly extinguished, and the rest of that noble pile, which had cost so many ages in erecting, preserved from destruction.[21]

Though Gulliver's quick thinking saves the palace, its long-term effects are less successful: the empress is repelled by his action and vows her revenge, and he only narrowly escapes being executed for high treason. Perhaps Swift was inspired by the story of the Sienese gentleman who engaged in therapeutic fire-fighting, and found his cure as he emptied his over-full bladder.

Renaissance melancholic delusions are flamboyant, theatrical affairs. As we have seen, from the case of the pissing Sienese gentleman to the Swiss man with a gut full of frogs, both the delusions and their cure require movements, props, and a cast of supporting characters. To revisit al-Razi's three degrees of symptoms, these melancholics think their delusion, they speak it, and they perform it. And they make energetic performances at that. It is no coincidence that the stories provided a rich source material for imaginative literature, from Tomkis' drama of the senses to Cervantes' fiction. Fantasies of breakability, delusions of power and prestige, and beliefs about failed bodily function allow melancholics to express fears and desires and enable writers and readers to explore the same. Melancholy opens up a different kind of insight into the world; its very strangeness gives the sufferer licence to reject social norms, to speak the unvarnished truth, and to see through pretence. In the next chapter, we will turn to a special category of mental disorder in which delusional symptoms are often present: erotic melancholy.

FIGURE 5.1 Jacques Ferrand, *Erotomania* (1640).

5
Love and Sex

When the Polish physician Józef Struś (Struthius, 1510–68) visited one of his patients, the wife of a nobleman, he knew he had to try an unusual method to diagnose what was wrong with her. The woman's husband was away on a journey and Struś was charged with treating her for a fever. But he realised that the cause of her ailment was more than simply physical.

He did what any doctor might do at a consultation: he took her pulse. But Struś had an inkling that the woman's sickness was emotional in origin, and that she had fallen in love with another man. As he held her wrist and felt the arterial flow, he contrived a method to test his theory. During the course of his bedside conversation, he dropped in the names of as many men in her circle as he knew. Her pulse remained steady until he got to one man's name, when he noticed a sudden change. The ordinary pace of her heart started to vary; it beat faster and its rhythm became disrupted, sometimes weaker, sometimes stronger. Thus Struś not only confirmed that she was in love, but with whom.[1]

What gave the noblewoman's secret away was the *pulsus amatorius*: the pulse of love. Struś was a specialist in the heartbeat who wrote a diagnostic textbook on the pulse, the *Ars sphygmica* (1540), teaching his students to recognise five basic types and to look for any changes in rhythm which might indicate an underlying condition.[2] That could include passionate emotion. When he diagnosed his female patient, he drew on a long tradition of medical authorities from Galen through to a whole host of medieval and Renaissance physicians, who held that love sickness could be diagnosed through bodily signs, of which the *pulsus amatorius* was a major indicator. Others included a pale face, sleep loss, blushing at the name of the beloved, sweating, and shivering. While Sir Philip Sidney wrote of lovers who were afflicted with 'freezing fires', a staple of the Petrarchan sonnet tradition, Galenic physicians saw the idea as a medical reality.[3]

For Robert Burton and his contemporaries, love sickness was more than simply metaphorical. Several Renaissance medical textbooks include chapters about charting the effects of human desire on physical and mental health. A whole separate category of melancholy was love or 'heroic' melancholy, named for one of several reasons (writers were not agreed on which): perhaps because it was a disease of heroes, or afflicted socially elevated people more commonly than labouring men and women; or perhaps because it was derived from the name of Eros, the Greek god of love, meaning the same as 'erotic'. The French physician Jacques Ferrand devoted a whole book to the subject, *De la maladie d'amour, ou mélancolie érotique* (1623) ('Of love sickness, or erotic melancholy'), the English version of which was entitled *Erotomania* (Figure 5.1). The boundary between simply being in love and suffering from the disease of love melancholy was a porous one: Burton, Ferrand, and their contemporaries drew on poetry and drama to inform their descriptions of the effects of desire, and much of their writing

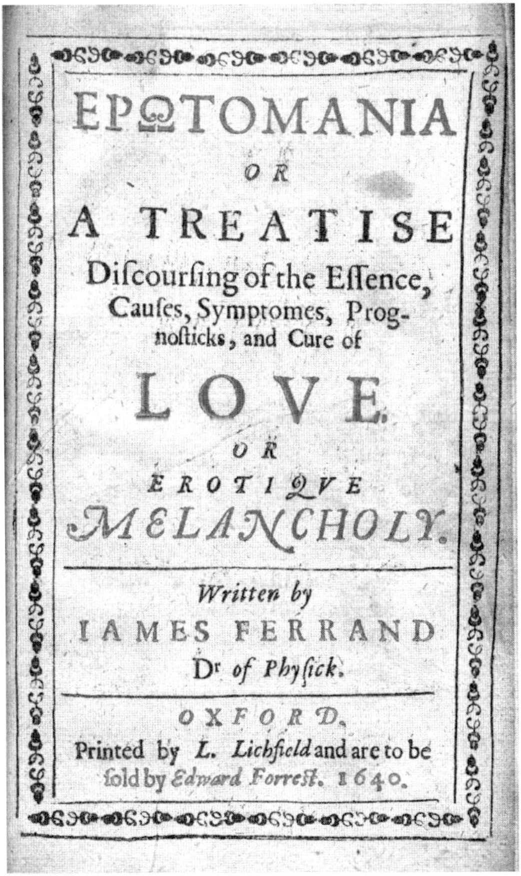

ΕΡΩΤΟΜΑΝΙΑ
OR
A TREATISE
Diſcourſing of the Eſſence,
Cauſes, Symptomes, Prog-
noſticks, and Cure of
LOVE.
OR
EROTIQVE
MELANCHOLY.

Written by
IAMES FERRAND
Dr of Phyſick.

OXFORD,
Printed by L. Lichfield and are to be
ſold by Edward Forreſt. 1640.

FIGURE 5.2 *The Foure Complexions: Melancholy.* Engraving attrib. William Marshall (1662).

has a lightness of touch which suggests that their aim is to entertain as much as analyse a medical condition. Nonetheless, their works also show how love and sexual appetite could become an affliction with serious consequences for the body and mind, even inducing madness, delusion, and frenzy.

In this chapter we will explore how human desire came to be seen as a distinctive feature of the melancholic condition, breaking the boundaries of social decorum and revealing itself through strange, and occasionally embarrassing, symptoms. In order to do that, we will first address how melancholy was gendered. So far in this book, the majority of our case histories have been of male sufferers; cases of female melancholy are harder to find in the medical literature but, as the case of the nobleman's wife shows us, they are not altogether absent. Women's physiology was seen to have a close connection to their distinctive experience of this condition, and sexual activity – or the lack of it – was often perceived to be at the heart of female melancholic experience.

Women's melancholy

Though women who suffered from the disease are more scarce than men in the medical literature, melancholy itself is a female figure (Figure 5.2). The Latinised Greek word *melancholia* is a feminine noun, and melancholy's deep association with the contemplative, as opposed to the active, life connects it with Renaissance ideas of feminised behaviour. In Albrecht Dürer's 'Melencolia I' (Figure 5.3), it is a female winged figure who sits in a sad and meditative pose, surrounded by items symbolic of artistic skill, higher knowledge, time, death, and physical decay.

When Burton writes of his relationship with his subject-matter, he uses similar tropes. Melancholy is his muse – 'this malady, shall I say my mistress Melancholy …?' (i.21). But when he speaks of the sufferer, this person is more commonly imagined as male: 'I say of our

FIGURE 5.3 *Melancholy*. Johannes Wierix, after Albrecht Dürer (1602).

melancholy man, he is the cream of human adversity, the quintessence, and upshot' (i.434). Melancholy is the cruel, torturing female presence who torments men but whom they find impossible to resist.

Nonetheless, when he explores the question of who is likely to succumb to it, he follows the second-century Greek author Aretaeus in claiming that melancholics are 'of sexes both, but men more often; yet women misaffected are far more violent, and grievously troubled' (*Anatomy*, i.172). In Galenic terms, their predisposition towards being more severely affected by the passions and less ruled by reason accounts for the 'violence' with which they are assailed. There are several types of melancholy in which female suffering appears more prominently. One of these we have already seen in Chapter 3: the supernatural melancholy of devils and witchcraft, of the type that affected Katherine Gualter, was seen as more typically female; Brian Levack has estimated that at least three quarters of reported demoniacs in early modern Europe were women.[4] And another is the type of melancholy connected with sex and love. Jacques Ferrand argues that women are 'far more subject to this passion, and more cruelly tormented with it, than men are'.[5] In particular, women who are not sexually active are prone to a variety which Burton calls 'Nuns', maids', and widows' melancholy'.

Burton summarises the distinguishing features of women's melancholy as 'a vexation of the mind, a sudden sorrow from a small, light, or no occasion, with a kind of still dotage and grief of some part or other, head, heart, breasts, sides, back, belly, etc. with much solitariness, weeping, distraction'. It is not necessarily a constant condition, but rather comes and goes by fits. Some of its signs can be seen externally on the body: for instance, rough skin on the elbows, knees, and knuckles. And inner symptoms such as heartburn and palpitations, a throbbing feeling on the back, swollen breasts, fainting spells, and feeling 'dry, thirsty, suddenly hot' are all distinctive indicators of female melancholy (i.415). It is striking that he makes no attempt to differentiate among these symptoms for different periods of life or conditions of women: symptoms we might associate with adolescence, the menstrual cycle, the menopause, or old age are all listed together. Again, women who have just given birth are recognised as prone to melancholy, but their experience is not treated separately by Burton from those who are going through puberty.

The reasons why women's stories of melancholy are heard less frequently in printed medical histories are bound up with the ways that male physicians classified women's symptoms, and the seriousness, or otherwise, with which their complaints were taken.[6] A further reason comes from the way women voice their experiences, for Burton claims that silence and inarticulacy are defining symptoms of female melancholy: 'Many of them cannot tell how to express themselves in words, or how it holds them, what ails them; you cannot understand them, or well tell what to make of their sayings; so far gone sometimes, so stupified and distracted, they think themselves bewitched, they are in despair' (i.416). Women's melancholy is a problem both of expression and of interpretation. On the one hand, women face barriers to speaking (whether it is in the nature of the disease, or in their reluctance to tell men what they are feeling); on the other, the words that they do use are not heard and understood. Burton's 'you' here is implied to be a male doctor, unable – or unwilling – to interpret what he is hearing. The same problem is not attributed to male patients. Men's melancholy is heard, even if what they say does not conform to conventional logic: they may be 'ridiculous to others, in all their gestures, actions, speeches' or 'witty & merry, conceited in discourse, pleasant' (i.400) but there is no sense that they face a fundamental barrier to representing their inner experience through language.

Problems of Flow

Why does melancholy affect women in distinctive ways? A fundamental factor, according to Galenic medicine, is that women's humoral temperaments are different from men's: female bodies are naturally cooler and moister. Born with less natural heat, women are more prone to severe symptoms of melancholy through the coldness of that humour. Burton cites an example of a melancholic widow in Venice who suffered from phlegm adust – the corrupt version of the cold, moist humour – and was 'fat and very sleepy' (i.400); another of a woman who became epileptic and blind through melancholy: both typical symptoms of the disease from 'a cold cause' (i.431). Female melancholy is rarely associated with a brilliant if wayward intellect of the sanguine melancholic, though a rare, self-professed exception later in the seventeenth century is the aristocratic poet Margaret Cavendish, Duchess of Newcastle (1623?–73), who styled herself as a melancholic, solitary genius.[7]

While the coolness of women is part of their predisposition, equally significant is the way their bodies flow, or fail to flow. In healthy human bodies, the four humours and fluids taken in and out move in a way that is regular, moderate, and unobstructed. We ingest food and drink and our digestive system converts it into nourishment for the body. We sweat, urinate, defecate, menstruate, cry, have sex, sneeze, and spit, expelling our humours outwards. If we do these things in moderation and our humours are properly balanced, then our health remains stable. But too much or too little of any of these activities, or a stoppage or block, and our bodies risk becoming unhealthy.

Because women menstruate, according to Galenic physiology their bodies are more vulnerable to humoral imbalance. When girls reach puberty, when women have irregular cycles, when they give birth, and when their periods end, their regular flow is disrupted and those physical changes affect the proportions of their humours and make them more vulnerable to disease. 'This feral malady' (as Burton describes women's melancholy) is caused by 'heart and brain offended with those vicious vapours which come from menstruous blood' (i.414). Renaissance medicine explains that this blood stays in the womb and becomes corrupt, letting off dangerous fumes that can damage the imagination. This is something that happens particularly to older women, but also to anyone who has no sexual activity. Hence it is prevalent among nuns, whose claims of visionary spiritual experience might be dismissed as an effect of too much solitude and of vapours ascending to the brain.

Yet, though Burton covers conventional territory here, he does something that other male writers on melancholy in the Renaissance do not: he reprimands himself for straying into territory that is beyond his personal experience and expresses pity for the women who are 'violently carried away with this torrent of inward humours'. He even stops himself from enquiring further, in a moment of self-deprecating autobiographical confession: 'But where am I? Into what subject have I rushed? What have I to do with nuns, maids, virgins, widows? I am a bachelor myself, and lead a monastic life in a college' (i.417). Even as he admits his lack of suitability and experience, he cannot resist making a bawdy joke: in this period, to 'have to do with someone' is to have sex with him or her.

Nonetheless, he does not quite stop:

> And yet I must and will say something more, add a word or two *in gratiam virginum et viduarum* [in favour of virgins and widows], in favour of all such distressed parties, in commiseration of their present estate. And as I cannot choose but condole their mishap that labour of this infirmity and are destitute of help in this case, so must I needs inveigh against them that are in fault. (i.418)

Burton's discussion of the medical causes and symptoms of female melancholy turns into a tirade against those who neglect, condemn, or reject women 'out of worldly respects, covetousness, supine negligence, their own private ends': hard-hearted parents who refuse to let their daughters marry the men they love; avaricious guardians; noble families more interested in dynastic alliances than in their children's happiness; cruel friends.

He lays blame for the woes of female melancholics at the door not just of individuals, but of structures of power. He attacks the 'stupid politicians' who make over-severe restrictive laws, and – in a conventional piece of Protestant diatribe – he rails against the 'rash vows of popish monasteries' (i.418). By imposing celibacy, these institutions and people also impose the risk of ill health and dangerous diseases upon both women and men. Given that one of those people who lived in enforced celibacy was Burton himself – since fellows of Oxford colleges were not allowed to marry – it is hard not to hear a personal inflection to his anger.

Sex

> Felix Plater, in the first book of his Observations, tells a story of an ancient gentleman in Alsatia, that "married a young wife, and was not able to pay his debts in that kind for a long time together, by reason of his several infirmities: but she, because of this inhibition of Venus, fell into a horrible fury, and desired every one that came to see her, by words, looks, and gestures, to have to do with her," etc.
>
> Jacchinus ... instanceth in a patient of his, that married a young wife in a hot summer, "and so dried himself with chamber-work, that he became in short space, from melancholy, mad": he cured him by moistening remedies.
>
> (i.235–6)

The twin stories retold by Burton from sixteenth-century physicians – the Swiss Felix Platter and the Italian Leonardo Giachini – show two sides of the same coin. Both involve poor nuptial matches, with a younger bride married to an older man, and both imply that the sexual appetites of young women have dangerous consequences. 'Venus' – Burton's word for sexual activity – is a risky business, whether it is inhibited or over-indulged and especially for an older person. But the victims of melancholy are different: in the first tale, the older groom's inability to satisfy his wife sent her into a fury where she broke the normal bounds of decency; in the second tale, it was the man who became deranged after he had used up his vital heat and moisture through 'chamber-work'. In the words of the Italian physician Antonio Guainerio (died 1440), sex 'infrigidates and dries up the body, consumes the spirits', so it is especially to be avoided if someone is already of a cold and dry constitution.

As we have seen in the discussion of menstruation, the retention of humours and of 'seed' (which women as well as men were believed to carry) was behind a great deal of melancholic distress, while, at the other extreme, too much evacuation of the same was equally damaging. Sex, like any other activity that evacuates fluid, needs to be moderated. Too little – such as in the abstinence practised by nuns and priests, widows and widowers – and one might fall into 'grievous melancholy' (i.235), just as one might from blocked bowels or stopping of monthly periods, with symptoms such as 'heaviness' of mind and headaches. On the other hand, too much can lead to the same result, in the same way that too much bloodletting or diarrhoea or vomiting might cause mental distress.

While excessive sexual activity is one potential cause of melancholy, it can also be a symptom. Those who suffer from hypochondriacal melancholy (the type that relates to the organs of the abdomen including the liver, spleen, guts, womb, and stomach) are particularly prone towards having an excessive sexual appetite. This is because they tend to have an overheated liver – the seat of sexual passion – or because, in the case of women, their melancholy is related to troubles of the uterus. Jacques Ferrand considers all erotic melancholy to be 'flatuous' or hypochondriacal in origin. He explains the physiological reasons why those who suffer from it, and those who have an excess of blood adust, have more sex than others:

[They] are hot and dry, and apt to have engendered within them a certain kind of flatulent vapour, that tickles them extremely, and by consequent, makes them beyond measure lascivious ... Besides, those that are melancholy by reason of the adustion of pure blood, have their imagination for the most part very strong: by the force of which a man oftentimes is incontinent, and by fancying the pleasure to himself enjoys it really.[8]

Ferrand's explanation shows just how closely body and mind were thought to work in interrelationship in Renaissance medicine. If flatulence seems to us an unlikely cause of (or excuse for) lascivious behaviour, Ferrand's humoral argument was widely accepted; indeed, it originates in Galen's commentary on Hippocrates' *Epidemics*. As we have seen in the previous chapter, melancholy is a disease of the imagination in which delusion often plays a part. Vivid fantasy is part of the unrestrained thoughts and behaviour of the delusional, 'incontinent' – that is to say, sexually uncontrolled – melancholic man, or indeed woman. The young wife from Alsatia whose elderly husband could not give her sexual satisfaction became unable to restrain her desire, until she propositioned anyone she saw; her lascivious behaviour would have been seen as a problem both of her womb and of her diseased imagination.

A 'ticklish' sexual appetite may have its advantages. Like Ferrand, the Dutch physician Jason van de Velde (Pratensis) observes that those suffering from the hypochondriacal variety of the disease desire sex more than others, but that sexual activity also has the therapeutic effect of relieving their flatulence (i.413). The way that this happens may nonetheless be rather unfortunate. Hippocrates records several cases of patients who suffered from intestinal gas and rumbling noises during sex.[9] Perhaps this is one reason why the Earl of Montfort, whom we met in Chapter 2, was advised to have only moderate sexual activity, and never after a meal.

The Look of Love

How can you spot a sufferer of erotic melancholy? At the start of this chapter, we saw how a woman was diagnosed through the rhythm of her pulse. But visual clues are also striking indicators of the disorder. Love melancholics have a distinctive look. Their eyes – 'love's orators', as Petronius called them (iii.83) – are typically downcast, as they muse on the object of their affection and withdraw into themselves. Jacques Ferrand even calls the eye muscle that makes them look downwards the 'musculus amorosus' (the amorous muscle).[10] The further they are lost to love, the more extreme their appearance. Those who are severely afflicted by their passion become hollow-eyed, as well as thin and dry in their bodies since their appetite wanes. They look as if they are pining away, lost in their contemplations of their beloved, and they have a tendency to sigh and cry (iii.133).

They can also be recognised through their distinctive colouring. While all melancholics can be pale, those suffering from heroic melancholy have a particular hue which Ferrand describes as the 'badge of love': a mixed white, yellow, and green on the skin. One of the examples he finds for this comes, not from a medical casebook, but from Ovid's *Metamorphoses*. The water nymph Clytie pined away for the love of the sun god Sol, neither eating nor drinking as she lay on the ground, weeping. At last, 'her limbs grew fast to the soil and her deathly pallor changed in part to a bloodless plant', the heliotrope.[11] That combination of paleness and a green tinge is characteristic of sufferers.

This phenomenon has a physiological explanation. Ferrand describes how this distinctive pale colour 'is caused by the permixtion of yellow choler with the thin waterish parts of the blood', these humours becoming corrupt and then revealing themselves in the skin.[12] Burton's description of this symptom, taken from Jason van de Velde (Pratensis), suggests similar physical origins:

> because of the distraction of the spirits the liver doth not perform his part, nor turns the aliment into blood as it ought, and for that cause the members are weak for want of sustenance, they are lean and pine, as the herbs of my garden do this month of May, for want of rain. (iii.133)

Van de Velde's analogy of lovers to his wilting plants echoes the fate of Clytie. The burning desire which love ignites stops the liver from performing its normal function, which in turn creates the greenish-yellow colour on the skin.[13] Though Ferrand and Burton ascribe this distinctive skin tone to love melancholics of both sexes, it was particularly associated with young women after puberty, seen to suffer from 'green sickness', a condition that was taken as a sign that they were in need of sexual activity and should be found a husband. Romeo, seeing Juliet at her balcony by the light of the moon, wishes that Juliet may no longer be the moon's maid – that is, remain a virgin – since 'Her vestal livery is but sick and green / And none but fools do wear it. Cast it off.'[14] Romeo's speech probably does not come from a concern for Juliet's liver function, but the green sickness nonetheless has its origins in that organ.

Though heroic melancholy is not always easy to spot, its visual clues can reveal the disease to a well-informed physician. Such was the case for Jacques Ferrand when he first started to practise medicine in Agen, in south-west France. He was called upon to treat a young scholar with a mysterious ailment. He complained that he could not sleep 'nor take delight in anything in the world' despite all the medicines that many physicians had prescribed him. He had even moved from Toulouse to Agen, in the hope that a change of air would revive his spirits, but found himself even more discontented than before. Ferrand assessed the man and took into account the fact that he was young, that he had previously been cheerful and merry, and that there was no apparent cause of his grief:

> [I] perceived withal his countenance to be grown pale, yellowish, and of a sad decayed colour; his eyes hollow; and all the rest of [his] body in reasonable good plight [condition]: I began to suspect it was some passion of the mind that thus tormented him: and then considering his age, and his complexion, which was sanguine, and his profession; I certainly concluded that his disease was love. And as I was urgent upon him to let me know the external cause of his malady, there comes by chance a handsome servant-maid of the house about some business or other into the room where we were, and was the means of discovering the true ground of his disease. For she coming in at the instant as I was feeling his pulse, I perceived it suddenly vary its motion, and beat very unequally; he presently grew pale, and blushed again in a moment, and could hardly speak.[15]

As with the noblewoman treated by Józef Struś, it was the *pulsus amatorius* – the lover's pulse – that finally gave the patient away and enabled Ferrand to diagnose what was wrong with him. Yet it was the signs in his face, particularly his colouring and his eyes, that first pointed Ferrand towards the nature of his disease. The 'badge of love' is not only a woman's complaint. Gathering together the evidence, Ferrand was able to deduce that the man did not suffer from ordinary melancholy, but the erotic version that is typical among people of his age and humoral predisposition.

Symptoms in the Mind

While these physical signs are characteristic indicators of love melancholy, other, inner symptoms are also typical. Fear and sorrow, the great hallmarks of melancholy, are often found in lovers as they become suspicious and jealous, stricken by shyness in front of their beloved, or as they pine away when their feelings are unrequited or unfulfilled: 'Shall I say, most part of a lover's life is full of agony, anxiety, fear, and grief, complaints, sighs, suspicions, and cares (heigh-ho, my heart is woe), full of silence and irksome solitariness?' (iii.143–4). Burton's tone here is playful: for him, love is a 'tragi-comedy' that demands a 'mixed tone', sometimes satirical, sometimes serious or comic as the subject gives occasion (iii.10). If the lover's symptoms can be grave, they can also make him look ridiculous – like *Twelfth Night*'s Malvolio in his cross-gartered yellow stockings, or the 'Inamorato' pictured on the frontispiece of *The Anatomy of Melancholy* (Figure 0.1).

Like other kinds of melancholic, those who suffer from the heroic kind have a propensity towards delusions, often connected with the sight. Renaissance love is a famously visual phenomenon: according to Platonic theory, the eyes emit rays in order to perceive objects; when two people fall in love, each person's eyes cast out beams which enter the other person's and project an image of the beloved within. As Marsilio Ficino explains it, commenting on Plato, 'Mortal men are then especially bewitched, when as by often gazing one on the other, they direct sight to sight, join eye to eye, and so drink and suck in love between them; for the beginning of this disease is the eye' (iii.85).[16] The images of love as witchcraft and as an infection transmitted through sight are as widespread in poetry as they are in Platonic philosophy.

The act of melancholic loving is one of prolonged looking; outer behaviour comes to reflect a state of inner obsession. By way of example, Burton recounts a Pygmalion-like story from the Lucianic *Amores* of a young man who fell in love with a picture of the goddess Venus, and visited her temple every day to look at it, sitting in front of it from morning till night (iii.139). While this case suggests love prompted by art, the love melancholic cannot keep from looking at the object of his affection, even when she is no longer physically present:

> her sweet face, eyes, actions, gestures, hands, feet, speech, length, breadth, height, depth, and the rest of her dimensions, are so surveyed, measured, and taken, by that astrolabe of phantasy, and that so violently sometimes, with such earnestness and eagerness, such continuance, so strong an imagination, that at length he thinks he sees her indeed; he talks with her, he embraceth her. (iii.148)

The workings of his imagination are so strong that he becomes convinced his beloved is with him everywhere he goes. Several case histories tell of men afflicted with this disorder, which is suggestive of the gendered nature of this particular delusion. The beloved female object is measured by the male lover's gaze, whose imagination operates like a surveying instrument to take in and store her dimensions and reproduce them to his mind's eye.

In the way Burton describes it, this visual delusion has something in common with the Petrarchan blazon, where a woman is poetically praised through a detailed description of her body from her hair downwards. Indeed, the French physician André du Laurens' description of the heroic melancholic's deluded thinking seems to be inspired by the conventions of Petrarchan sonneteering:

> he seemeth to himself to see long golden locks, finely frizzled and curled with a thousand rounds and winding twirls; a high brow, like unto the bright heavens, white and smooth, like the polished alablaster; two stars standing in the head very clear, resembling the beautiful flowers.[17]

Perhaps the heroic melancholic has absorbed these poetic stereotypes into his own imaginative processes; whether the object of his affections bears any resemblance to the ideal beauty depicted here is open to question.

Burton locates delusion in the very way that lovers perceive the one whom they adore. He strays far from the territory of melancholy as he describes love's blindness, in a passage so wildly excessive that it can only be quoted at length:

> Every lover admires his mistress, though she be very deformed of herself, ill-favoured, wrinkled, pimpled, pale, red, yellow, tanned, tallow-faced, have a swollen juggler's platter face, or a thin, lean, chitty face, have clouds in her face, be crooked, dry, bald, goggle-eyed, blear-eyed, or with staring eyes, she looks like a squis'd cat, hold her head still awry, heavy, dull,

hollow-eyed, black or yellow about the eyes, or squint-eyed, sparrow-mouthed, Persian hook-nosed, have a sharp fox nose, a red nose, China flat, great nose, *nare simo patuloque* [snub and flat nose], a nose like a promontory, gubber-tushed, rotten teeth, black, uneven, brown teeth, beetle-browed, a witch's beard, her breath stink all over the room, her nose drop winter and summer, with a Bavarian poke under her chin, a sharp chin, lave-eared, with a long crane's neck, which stands awry too, *pendulis mammis* [pendulous breasts], "her dugs like two double jugs", or else no dugs, in that other extreme, bloody-fallen fingers, she have filthy, long unpared nails, scabbed hands or wrists, a tanned skin, a rotten carcass, crooked back, she stoops, is lame, splay-footed, "as slender in the middle as a cow in the waist," gouty legs, her ankles hang over her shoes, her feet stink, she breed lice, a mere changeling, a very monster, an oaf imperfect, her whole complexion savours, a harsh voice, incondite gesture, vile gait, a vast virago, or an ugly tit, a slug, a fat fustilugs, a truss, a long lean rawbone, a skeleton, a sneaker (*si qua latent meliora puta* [think that what is not seen is better]), and to thy judgment looks like a mard [turd] in a lantern, whom thou couldst not fancy for a world, but hatest, loathest, and wouldst have spit in her face, or blow thy nose in her bosom, *remedium amoris* [a cure for love] to another man, a dowdy, a slut, a scold, a nasty, rank, rammy, filthy, beastly quean, dishonest peradventure, obscene, base, beggarly, rude, foolish, untaught, peevish, Irus' daughter, Thersites' sister, Grobian's scholar; if he love her once, he admires her for all this, he takes no notice of any such errors, or imperfections of body or mind … he had rather have her than any woman in the world. (iii.155–6)

Burton revels in repulsiveness, delighting in the sheer excess of his scorn. His misogynist diatribe is Rabelaisian in its grotesque, earthy energy. Even though his list encompasses all the extreme physical attributes that a woman might possibly have ('though she be ... ' is a subjunctive, a contraction of 'though she might be'), the cumulative effect is to make the reader imagine a woman in which all of these attributes are present at once, even the impossible ones – like all the alternative shapes of her nose. This mistress is an opposite to the Petrarchan ideal of womanhood, but Burton's joke is that the love-blind man can see none of her flaws.

Worshipping the beauty of one's beloved and imagining her or him as present may be a hallmark symptom of being in love. But one further consequence of this adoration is 'not lightly to be overpassed, that likely of what condition soever, if once they be in love, they turn to their ability, rhymers, ballet-makers, and poets' (iii.179). Writing love poetry is a symptom of illness, Burton suggests. It is not enough simply to admire another person's physical attributes, but love melancholy forces the afflicted person to compose ballads and rhymes. Du Laurens' description of the idealised woman as she appears in the mind of the love melancholic is halfway towards a sonnet, with her 'golden locks' and eyes like 'two stars'; the lover cannot help but cast his (deluded) thoughts into poetic form.

Burton is particularly scathing about those 'ancient men' who fall in love and start writing bad poetry, as the heat of love will 'thaw their frozen affections, dissolve the ice of age, and so far enable them, though they be sixty years of age above the girdle, to be scarce thirty beneath' (iii.179). And we may think of Benedick in *Much Ado About Nothing* – a play Burton mentions in his discussion of the causes of melancholy (iii.103) – trying to write a love song for Beatrice and bemoaning his failure to find appropriate line endings: 'Marry, I cannot show it in rhyme … No, I was not born under a rhyming planet nor I cannot woo in festival terms.'[18] Love makes people ridiculous, and bad poetry is hardly a victimless crime.

Then again, Burton's discussion of the causes, symptoms, and cures of heroic melancholy is punctuated with love poetry quoted from the classics, from Chaucer and Shakespeare. His writing is a celebration of the energy and creative zest that love inspires:

> This love is the cause of all good conceits, neatness, exornations, plays, elegancies, delights, pleasant expressions, sweet motions and gestures, joys, comforts, exultancies, and all the sweetness of our life … This love is that salt that seasoneth our harsh and dull labours, and gives a pleasant relish to our other unsavoury proceedings. (iii.181)

It may make us behave foolishly or even make us mad, but its cruelties, griefs, joys, and elation are also the prompt for art, poetry, and music. Artistic creation is boundless because 'there is no end of love's symptoms, 'tis a bottomless pit' (iii.184).

This celebratory mode extends, at last, to the cures of love. There are ways to try and dampen lustful passions and melancholic yearnings: André du Laurens recommends a change of air, abundant physical exercise outdoors, broths with almond milk, and perhaps opiates to cheer up the heart. A disciplined, abstemious diet also helps, as does simply separating the patient from the person he or she desires.[19] But all writers agree on one fail-safe remedy. In Burton's words, 'the last and best cure of love-melancholy is, to let them have their desire' (iii.228). According to Ibn Sina, it is the quickest way of restoring health: a man who has wasted away to skin and bones may rapidly recover once he has married. Fulfilled love brings joy and renewed energy. It may not cure foolish behaviour, but, Burton reflects, at least a pair of lovers will be happy in their foolishness: 'they may then kiss and coll, lie and look babies in one another's eyes, as their sires before them did; they may then satiate themselves with love's pleasures, which they have so long wished and expected' (iii.229).

From the joys of fulfilled love, we turn in the next chapter towards the opposite extreme: the agony of despair – a sign, perhaps, of how all-encompassing *The Anatomy of Melancholy* is of the range of human emotional experience. As we have seen in Chapter 3, Burton made special categories not only of love melancholy but also of religious melancholy. This last type is closely related to love melancholy, for, he argues, all human misery stems from 'how we mistake, wander and swerve' from the love of God (iii.313). In the case of one man – Francis Spira – his complete loss of hope in divine mercy led to a case of despair that was not only fatal, but became notorious across Protestant Europe.

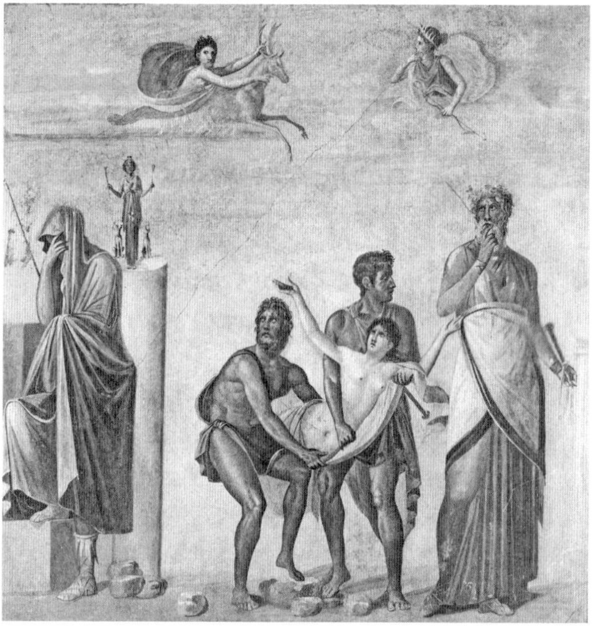

FIGURE 6.1 Fresco in the National Museum of Naples, depicting the sacrifice of Iphigenia. Alinari (c. 1875 – c. 1900).

6
Despair

What, therefore, Timanthes did in his picture of Iphigenia,
now ready to be sacrificed, when he had painted Calchas
mourning, Ulysses sad, but most sorrowful Menelaus, and
showed all his art in expressing variety of affections,
he covered the maid's father Agamemnon's head with a veil,
and left it to every spectator to conceive what he would himself;
for that true passion and sorrow in *summo gradu*, such as his was,
could not by any art be deciphered: what he did in his picture,
I will do in describing the symptoms of despair.

(Burton, *Anatomy*, iii.404)

For the author of *The Anatomy of Melancholy*, there is no mental pain like despair. So sharp is the suffering it brings that Robert Burton turns to visual art to hint at its extent. The ancient Greek painter Timanthes depicted the scene in Homer's *Iliad* (also the subject of a play by Euripides) when the Greeks are about to carry out the demand of the goddess Artemis: they must sacrifice the young princess Iphigenia in order to appease the deity's anger, so that she will make the winds favourable for the Greek fleet to sail to Troy (Figure 6.1). The grief-stricken face of Iphigenia's father, King Agamemnon, remains hidden in the painting because it is beyond the expressive powers of art.

So likewise is despair: all Burton can do as he attempts to describe its symptoms is to heap up words, knowing that they are inadequate to bear the load: 'imagine what thou canst, fear, sorrow, furies, grief, pain, terror, anger, dismal, ghastly tedious, irksome, etc. it is not sufficient, it comes far short, no tongue can tell, no heart conceive it'. It is this subject that we will explore in this chapter, through a single case history mentioned in the *Anatomy* and many other places. The story of Francis Spira (1502–48), the man who succumbed to despair by believing that he was damned, was so infamous that it haunted the imagination of Protestant Europe during the sixteenth century and for several centuries after.

Defining Despair

Burton writes about despair at the very end of the *Anatomy*, perhaps because it is the most extreme form of mental affliction he knows. He defines it as 'a sickness of the soul without any hope or expectation of amendment' (iii.392). Whereas other diseases of the body and mind find some kind of remedy, what medicine can treat this, he asks? And while melancholics may be comforted and quietened in mind, 'who can put to silence the voice of desperation?' It presents a challenge for physicians and clergymen alike. Hope of recovery is small because it is a condition marked by hope's absence: those who suffer from it can see no way out. Not just the worst of afflictions, it is like all of them combined: ''Tis an epitome of hell, an extract, a quintessence, a compound, a mixture of all feral maladies, tyrannical tortures, plagues, and perplexities' (iii.404).

Perhaps the most recurrent image used to conjure what it means to feel despair is being in hell itself. Speaking out of the midst of it, one sufferer whose story we shall follow

FIGURE 6.2 *Melancholic Temperament*. Harmen Jansz Muller, after Maarten van Heemskerck (1566).

in this chapter tells his friends what it is like for him: 'We that are drowned in the pit in despair, are dead and are already gone down into the pit.'[1] It is more like being dead already than it is like living, even a life of illness. For Burton and his contemporaries, despair is a spiritual experience: more than hopelessness, it is living under a continual sense of God's anger, without any promise of release through God's mercy. A touchstone for writers and sufferers is the penitential Psalms:

O Lord, rebuke me not in thy wrath: neither chasten me in thy hot displeasure.
For thine arrows stick fast in me, and thy hand presseth me sore.

There is no soundness in my flesh because of thine anger;
neither is there any rest in my bones because of my sin.
For mine iniquities are gone over mine head: as an heavy
burden they are too heavy for me. (Psalms 38:1–4)

Psalms such as this one lent scriptural support for the idea that spiritual suffering may be a necessary part of the salvific process and authorised a language for expressing mental and spiritual pain; their influence can be found widely in Renaissance writing about the afflicted conscience.[2]

Is despair the same as melancholy? The question opens up contested territory in the Renaissance. As we will see, for many writers the two afflictions are quite separate, but Burton's inclusion of 'Despair' as the final section of *The Anatomy of Melancholy* makes a bold case that they share common ground. While despairing is mental and spiritual, it also has physical manifestations: the psalmist provides a compelling vocabulary for this anguish as being written on the body in a sense of inner wounding, in the flesh's wasting away, and in pain that penetrates even to the bones. These are more than metaphors because they acknowledge that mental pain is transmitted into physical terms. In those who despair, Burton says, 'fear takes away their content, and dries the blood, wasteth the marrow, alters their countenance' (iii.405): signs that are classic manifestations of melancholy too. And despair often leads to suicide, as suggested by men hanging themselves in Harmen Jansz Muller's illustration of the melancholic temperament (Figure 6.2).

The experience of despair may be another dimension of the symptoms of black bile and of the fumes from corrupt humours ascending to the brain, according to Galenic physicians. Then again, these same symptoms may be the signs of a conscience in crisis, for which the ointments and purges of Galenic medicine can do no good at all. The idea of despair stands on the boundaries of religion and medicine in the sixteenth and seventeenth centuries, and the question of how to treat those suffering from it puts ideas about the interrelationship of body, mind, and soul to the test.[3]

The Death of Francis Spira

The fearful story of Francis Spira (as he was known in England; Francesco Spiera in Italian) was first recounted in an eye-witness account by a man who was present at his deathbed, Matteo Gribaldi. It was commented upon by Jean Calvin, was retold in Latin and several European languages including English, was recast into a ballad, and even found new expression in Christopher Marlowe's tragic theatre and the spiritual autobiography of John Bunyan.[4] Spira's death is more than a case history of a melancholic. It is the tale of a man who became internally riven by the wounds of religious and political schism. His spiritual doubt grew into terrifying, self-destroying certainty, and his desperate end became a cautionary tale for others about the dangers of apostasy. Spira's name became a byword for irredeemable reprobation, spoken of in the same breath as Cain and Judas – and the first person who made that damning assocation was Spira himself.

Spira was a civil lawyer who lived in Citadella in northern Italy, not far from Padua. The area was in the territory of the Venetian Republic, the heartland of Italian religious reform: Venice and Padua were gathering points for Italian Protestants in the early years after Martin Luther's ideas spread across Europe, although – as we will see – they were hardly places of safety. Married with eleven children, Spira was a wealthy and well-respected citizen who held a high reputation for learning and eloquence.

When Spira was forty-four, he first became exposed to the writings of Luther. After studying them for some time, Spira converted from Roman Catholicism to Protestantism, and not only that: he proceeded to teach these new opinions to his wife, family, friends, and fellow citizens. Over the course of four years he promulgated Protestant doctrine ever more widely; as one English account of his story puts it, 'this fire could not keep itself within private walls, but at length it brake forth into public meetings' and he became a prominent voice of the new religious reforming movement throughout the region.[5]

In so doing, he came to the attention of the local Roman Catholic hierarchy. A papal legate ordered him to appear before the Inquisition in Venice. Spira knew exactly what this meant. Either he would have to apostasise, publicly recanting his Protestantism, or he would face persecution: the loss of all his wealth, harm to his family, imprisonment, exile – and possibly even death itself. Faced with this intolerable dilemma, Spira chose to recant. Yet this was not a simple matter of giving the Inquisition his assurance that he was now loyal to the authority of the Catholic Church. The papal legate made Spira sign a document describing his errors, abjuring as heresy the doctrines taught by Luther and declaring his obedience to the Church of Rome. Then he commanded

Spira to return to his home town and read the document out loud in public.

On the journey home and wracked with guilt and shame, Spira thought he heard a voice from heaven calling out to him, as Saul did on the road to Damascus: 'Spira, what doest thou here, whither goest thou? … dost thou well in preferring wife and children before Christ?'[6] Spira was full of doubts about what to do, but the voice assured him that 'the gate of mercy is not quite shut' and that there was still a chance for him to repent and save his soul. Arriving home, he confessed all to his friends and asked their advice. They recommended that it would not be wise to put the safety of his family and friends – themselves included, of course – at any further risk. The next morning at the end of mass, Spira stood up in front of two thousand people and read out loud his declaration.

Though he had saved himself and his circle from persecution and (perhaps) martyrs' deaths, Spira's torment had only just begun. The moment he left the church, he heard a voice once again. This time, its tone was terrible: 'Hence Apostate, bear with thee the sentence of eternal damnation.'[7] He collapsed in the street. Those friends who had advised him to recant rallied round him, but he assured them that there was nothing they could do for him: he had been judged by God and was utterly undone. All hope was lost.

As they tried to assure him that it was just his imagination, some of his friends blamed his melancholic constitution for producing these symptoms. They took him to the best doctors in Padua for medical treatment. After the physicians had examined him, they agreed on their diagnosis: Spira's illness arose from a grief of mind, which had stirred up bad humours in the body. These, 'ascending up into the brain, troubled the fancy, shadowed the seat of the judgement, and so corrupted it'. They prescribed a course of treatment that involved purging the bad humours from him, but it was all to no avail. Spira utterly rejected the therapies his doctors attempted to administer:

> Alas, poor men, how far wide are you; do you think that this disease is to be cured by potions? Believe me there must be another manner of medicine, it is neither potions, plasters, nor drugs, that can help a fainting soul cast down with sense of sin and the wrath of God; it is only Christ that must be the physician, and the Gospel the sole antidote.[8]

His body became a battleground for competing claims about where his spiritual and mental anguish had come from. Yet Spira himself was certain that what he was undergoing was not melancholy, but a just punishment for sins which God could no longer forgive. He was already in hell. He simply had not died yet.

While medical treatment brought no release, neither did spiritual consolation. Clergymen and friends prayed with him and tried to assure him that all was not lost: there was still time to repent, and God would be merciful to him, just as God was to the penitent thief who died next to Jesus on the cross. Spira rejected all these comforts. His case was unique, he insisted. He had denied Christ, he had 'a whole legion of devils that take up their dwelling within me', he had committed the unpardonable sin against the Holy Spirit of which Jesus had spoken (Matthew 12:31–2); no other case was like his. His heart was hardened, he told them, and he was accursed so that he could only feel God's wrath, like the torments of the damned: 'verily desperation is hell itself'.[9]

As his torments continued unabated, those around him tried more and more extreme remedies. A priest tried to exorcise him. A bishop brought him Holy Communion. Learned theologians tried to reason that they could see evidence of his salvation and that he need not give up hope. Spira was equal to every attempt, quoting line after line of scripture to show them that he was a reprobate and that he was eternally predestined to a grim fate. He became something of a cause célèbre: more and more people tried their hand at rescuing him from despair, or flocked to witness his agonies – a novel form of religious tourism – until his friends had to move him to escape the crowds.

His condition deteriorated beyond hope of recovery. On one occasion he snatched a knife that was lying on a table and was only just prevented from stabbing himself. Over eight weeks, he refused to eat anything until he was no more than skin and bones, though he 'vehemently raged for drink; ever pining, yet fearful to live long; dreaded hell, yet coveting death in a continual torment'.[10] At last he died, without expressing even a glimmer of hope for himself. One or two accounts suggest that he took his own life, but most of them imply that he simply wasted away.

The Haunting of Francis Spira

Spira's story took hold of the imaginations of European Protestants for several reasons. For one thing, it was a perfectly packaged warning about the dangers of abandoning the cause of Reformation. An agonising death on a pyre or a torturer's wheel might await those who accepted martyrdom, but what was the alternative? A fate like Spira's conjured up a vivid picture of the consequences of recanting in order to save one's life, or living as a Nicodemite (after Nicodemus in the Gospels, who visited Jesus in secret by night) and pretending loyalty to the Catholic Church while concealing one's true beliefs. The pamphlets that circulated about Spira's death express little sympathy for his pragmatic decision to yield to the Inquisition, and do not doubt that what he experienced was the authentic sign of God's judgement.

The utter relentlessness of Spira's inner collapse is a further, compelling element of his story. His battle against all the comforts other people try to offer him is as drawn-out as it is horrifying. As we read his story, we never forget that he was a highly trained lawyer, who could spot the weakness in every argument put forward by those people attempting to help him, and who responded to them with forensic efficiency and attention to detail. In his 'Symptoms of Despair', Robert Burton comments on this feature of his character: 'never pleaded any man so well for himself, as this man did against himself' (iii.407).

This reversal of the normal order of things – where Spira represents himself for the prosecution rather than the defence – makes for gripping, if painful, reading. He remorselessly turns the theology of predestination against himself. If, as Protestant doctrine has it, the actions of our lives are not causes of our final fate, but rather signs indicating whether we are already saved or damned, what if those signs suggest that we are destined for hell and we can do nothing to change it? Spira lives out the consequences of this question. At one point he turns the tables on the people who are trying to console him and becomes a kind of preacher to them, urging them to learn from his own misery and to be faithful even until death. One of them hazards to observe that 'these words … do not sound like the words of a wicked reprobate', but Spira will not allow himself even a chink of light: 'I do but here imitate … the rich glutton in the Gospel, who though in hell, yet was careful that his brethren should not come to that place of torment.'[11] Like Dives, the rich man who failed to help the beggar Lazarus at his gate, and who pleads in vain from hell that Lazarus might dip his finger in water and cool his tongue (Luke 16:19–31), Spira has left it too late, he claims. His deep knowledge of scripture means that he can retaliate against any comforts with chapter and verse, because quotations from the Bible can be used to condemn oneself just as much as they can to console.

A further reason why Spira's story gained such traction is that he speaks for himself, and does so at great length. In the case histories of Renaissance melancholy we have followed so far in this book, we rarely hear from the sufferers themselves. Occasionally their words are reported, but more commonly the perspective is that of the doctor or clergyman who treats their complaint. By contrast, Spira's voice is firmly at the centre of the narratives about him, and his speeches have an added layer of authenticity because they were originally reported by his friend (and eye-witness to his death) Matteo Gribaldi.[12]

Though these Protestant publications urge readers to interpret his fate as the judgement of God on a hardened sinner who denies Christ, they are also compelling for the insight they give into what it is like to feel despair. Spira is highly articulate, but his speeches are shot through with cries of pain:

> Then roaring out in the bitterness of his spirit, [he] said,
> It is a fearful thing to fall into the hands of the living God.

He casts himself as the protagonist of his own tragedy, saying that 'I am sure, I am not only the actor, but the argument, and matter of the tragedy'; he both performs his damnation and is the subject-matter of the drama he is enacting.[13]

This very performativity made the story ripe for theatrical adaptation, and it is not at all surprising that the figure of Spira made his way into Elizabethan drama. Nathaniel Woodes' *The Conflict of Conscience* (1581) tells Spira's story allegorically through the character of Philologus, a scholar who is a thinly veiled depiction of Spira. Yet it is another scholar who echoes Spira's voice even more strongly: the eponymous protagonist of that great tragedy of a soul in torment, Christopher Marlowe's *Dr Faustus* (first published 1604). The Wittenberg academic who has made a pact with Satan is convinced that his action puts him beyond God's mercy. Caught between his good and bad angels, Faustus (like Spira) attempts to pray, only to reject his own attempts as failure. His cries of spiritual agony – 'Ah, my God, I would weep! but the devil draws in my tears' – and the closed circle of his self-condemning mind are features he has in common with the Italian lawyer, and contribute towards creating the play's central tension and cathartic energy. Though we know that Faustus will die in despair and be dragged to hell by the devil Mephistopheles, each moment where he seems about to turn towards mercy seems balanced on a knife edge.[14]

The legacy of Spira's story survived far beyond the sixteenth century. It offered a compelling example of Calvinist predestination in action: the teaching that God determined from before the beginning of creation not only who is saved (or elect), but also who is damned (or reprobate), and all according to the secret workings of the divine will rather than any scheme that is discernible to humans. If we want to know whether we are elect or reprobate, we should look for the signs or 'fruit' in our lives.

John Bunyan's spiritual autobiography *Grace Abounding to the Chief of Sinners* (1666) shows the young man passing through all the same dark corridors of spiritual crisis as Francis Spira. He is convinced that he has committed the unforgivable sin, that he is worse than Judas, that the verses of scripture which keep jumping into his head – 'many are called but few are chosen' (Matthw 22:14); 'The man that sins presumptuously, shall be taken from God's altar, that he may die' (Exodus 21:14) – are all written for him. Even as 'despair was swallowing me up', he says, a book he comes across makes him even worse:

About this time I did light on that dreadful story of that miserable mortal *Francis Spira*, A Book that was to my troubled Spirit, as Salt when rubbed into a fresh wound; every Sentence in that book, every groan of that man, with all the rest of his actions in his dolors, as his tears, his prayers, his gnashing of teeth, his wringing of hands, his twineing and twisting, and languishing, and pineing away under that mighty hand of God that was upon him, was as Knives and Daggers in my Soul.

What causes Bunyan such agonies, above all, is not Spira's arguments but the vivid description of how he suffers. As a portrait of what it is like to be in a state of despair, Spira's story contains such a brutal authenticity that it holds up a mirror to Bunyan's own misery. Unlike Francis Spira, Bunyan's despair does not have a terrible end. Yet what makes him quite unique is his honest acknowledgement that, even as a mature preacher of the Gospel, he still oscillates between times of consolation and anguish: 'I have wondered much at this one thing, that though God doth visit my Soul with never so blessed a discovery of himself, yet I have found again, that such hours have attended me afterwards, that I have been in my spirit so filled with darkness.'[15] His is not a tale of conversion that brings peaceful inner contentment, but of a soul that lives half in shadow. His committed faith in God does not remove an inner anguish he still carries with him.

From Symptoms to Cure

Robert Burton uses Spira's story as one of his examples of the grave symptoms of despair. After *The Anatomy of Melancholy* was first published in 1621, it appeared in five further editions up until 1651. With each new edition, Burton was seemingly unable to stop adding to it. He inserted new case studies, stories, authorities, extra cures – and even, simply, more individual words. For the sixth edition – which only saw print eleven years after his death – he went through his text adding the word 'agony' to his descriptions of melancholy; age had not softened his depiction of the bitterness of melancholic affliction. The book grew in size by a third.[16]

But one small part of the *Anatomy* expanded far more radically than that. In the first edition, he ended 'Religious Melancholy' with a page of writing on 'Cure of Despair'. He told his readers that those people in desperate states should try to live moderately, should consult a physician, and should listen to the wise counsel of others, and he also recommended some works by theologians on the subject for them to read. In the second edition (1624), however, he extended the 'Cure of Despair' to twenty times its original length. This time, instead of instructing his reader to go and seek out other people's work, he turned the end of the *Anatomy* into a long consolation against despair.

The shift is a response to the seriousness of despair and its complexity. Like melancholy, it affects each person individually. Its symptoms vary from case to case: one person is as forensically logical as Francis Spira; another is reduced to fits of inarticulate raving; one sufferer will not dare to go near the river Rhine because of an overwhelming urge to throw himself in; another is tempted to curse God, blaspheme, and kill herself. Burton admits that 'some will hear good counsel, some will not; some desire help, some reject all, and will not be eased' (iii.408) – like Spira himself, of course.

He is candid that the prognostics for the despairing are not good. The man who fought an urge to jump in the Rhine eventually drowned himself. A merchant's wife with a long history of despair, treated by the Swiss doctor Felix Platter, at last got up in the night and threw herself from a high window into the street below. There are many similar stories in the annals of melancholy and Burton acknowledges that suicide – a word not yet introduced into English in Burton's day – is a probable outcome. Most theologians of the period would agree with Hamlet that the Everlasting had fixed his canon against self-slaughter, and that those who took their own lives would be damned because they died impenitent and without hope of God's mercy.[17]

Though Burton admits the logic of this argument when suicide results in instant death, he is anxious to offer a more charitable approach whenever possible. For one thing, perhaps the dying person may have even the briefest of opportunities to cry for mercy: God's forgiveness may slip in, even '*inter pontem et fontem*, *inter gladium et jugulum*, betwixt the bridge and the brook, the knife and the throat' (i.439). And for another, those who react uncharitably may be missing the fact that the victim was ill.

He tells a story from the casebooks of the Dutch physician Pieter van Foreest of two brothers who 'made away themselves'. The town condemned their desperate act and ordered that they should be 'infamously' buried outside consecrated ground, as a warning to others. But when it was revealed that they had been suffering from melancholy, the order was revoked and the brothers were given a duly solemn burial. They came to be seen as victims of illness, not perpetrators of a crime. Madness and melancholy take sufferers' wills away from them so that they are unable to make the right decisions, and Burton urges compassion for those who have ended their own lives: 'It is his case, it may be thine ... we ought not to be so rash and rigorous in our censures as some are; charity will judge and hope the best; God be merciful unto us all' (i.439).

Yet for all the worrying prognostics, Burton does not give up hope of relief for the despairing. His 'Cure of Despair' is addressed directly to those who suffer from it, and the first thing he asserts is that multitudes overcome despair, find the help they need, and are rescued 'from the chops of hell, and out of the devil's paws' (iii.409). He even mentions a story of a monk who was cured of despair with the help of medicine alone, though he adds that most people 'take a wrong course that think to overcome this feral passion by sole physic; and they are as much out, that think to work this effect by good advice alone … they must go hand in hand to this disease' (iii.409).

By suggesting that medicine has any effect at all, Burton swims against the current of most theological writers of his generation, who argue that the experience of a wounded conscience is separate from melancholy and can only be cured through spiritual advice, moral self-scrutiny, and repentance. The physician (and later minister) Timothy Bright, whose *Treatise of Melancholy* (1586) is the major English predecessor to the *Anatomy*, draws a sharp distinction. When the conscience is afflicted, 'no medicine, no purgation, nor cordial, no treacle or balm are able to assure the afflicted soul and trembling heart, now panting under the terrors of God'; but in a case of melancholy, 'the vein opened, sneezing powder or bear's foot ministered, cordials of pearl, sapphires, and rubies, with such like, recomfort the heart thrown down, and appalled with fantastical fear'.[18] Bright's words give us a foretaste of some of the medicinal treatments available in the Renaissance for melancholy. But those treatments do no good for cases of spiritual crisis.

By contrast, Burton – himself a clergyman – holds that black bile may be mixed in with anguish, and that despairing melancholics may be helped as much by fresh air and exercise as by a sermon. He even warns his afflicted readers that some of their misery may come from frightening themselves with certain types of religious practice. Whereas 'faith, hope, repentance, are the sovereign cures and remedies' (iii.426), listening to puritanical preachers can do more harm than good. For the sensitive soul, it is a wiser course of action to avoid books about predestination and ministers who strike terror into the hearts of their listeners with the flames of hellfire: 'let him read no more such tracts or subjects, hear no more such fearful tones, avoid such companies', but rather seek out good doctors and spiritual advisors who will minister to them with gentleness and compassion. They may 'ease his afflicted mind, relieve his wounded soul, and take him out of the jaws of hell itself' (iii.432).

The story of Spira has shown us a case of someone who turned out to be beyond cure, and – as we have seen so far – melancholy can in some cases turn out to be a lifelong, engrained condition, where containment may be the best hope available. For many, however, it is thoroughly treatable. In the next three chapters, we shall see the very varied methods by which Burton and physicians of the Renaissance treated this difficult, pervasive, and slippery, illness.

PART 3

CURES

7
The Non-Naturals

A young merchant going to Nordeling fair in Germany, for ten days' space never went to stool; at his return he was grievously melancholy, thinking that he was robbed, and would not be persuaded but that all his money was gone; his friends thought he had some philtrum given him, but Cnelius a physician being sent for, found his costiveness alone to be the cause, and thereupon gave him a clyster, by which he was speedily recovered.

(Burton, *Anatomy*, i.233–4)

The case history of melancholy recounted in the medical observations of the German writer Johann Schenck (1530/1–98) is a classic example of how much small physical changes can affect both the body and the mind. His young patient did not empty his bowels for so long that he became constipated (or 'costive'), perhaps because he was working at a fair where he was unable to find anywhere to relieve himself. This disruption to the normal flow of his body made its effects felt, not only within his body, but also in his thought processes: he became so delirious that (as Schenck notes) he hardly knew himself. While his friends thought he was the victim of a magic potion, his physician recognised that his delusion was a symptom of melancholy and treated it with an enema. His success was instant: by removing the physical obstruction, Schenck also healed his troubled mind.

This story illustrates a belief that is at the heart of Galenic medical teaching about the ways that the body and mind work together. Essential to human health are the six 'non-naturals', things which are not innate to the human body but which nonetheless affect it on a daily basis: our diet, the air we breathe, the substances we retain within or expel from our bodies, our exercise and rest, our sleeping and waking, and the passions to which our minds are subject. These non-naturals can vary not only from person to person but from day to day.

If we alter one of the non-naturals even a little, our normally good states of health may be knocked out of balance. The German merchant's constipation was a problem of the non-naturals known as 'retention and evacuation', and was cured quite simply by a bowel movement. Similarly, melancholics who stay in bed all day lost in their own thoughts – as melancholics tend to do – or stay up all night full of worries and fears may exacerbate their condition, while regulating their sleep to seven or eight hours (a time recommended then as now, ii.100) may be the key to curing them. In this chapter we will focus on three of the six non-naturals: diet, retention and evacuation, and exercise. The last of the non-naturals – the passions of the mind – is such an important topic in the treatment of melancholy that it merits separate attention in Chapter 9.

Prevention and Treatment

Renaissance therapies for melancholy are based on general rules tailored to individual circumstances, which rely on sufferers changing their behaviour and habits. They must moderate their habits, discipline themselves, and follow careful routines. They must get out of bed at a sensible time, defecate regularly, eat when they are hungry and not too much, do moderate exercise, and not stay up too late.

But this is easier said than done. Burton tells us that melancholics are naturally difficult patients. They have a tendency to be pessimistic about their own prospects of recovery. They are often neglectful of their health and hygiene, ignore worrying symptoms, and try to avoid medical treatment whenever they can. On the other hand, many are 'too profuse, suspicious, and jealous of their health, too apt to take physic on every small occasion, to aggravate every slender passion, imperfection, impediment' (ii.18). They tend to be impatient and restless, wanting to change doctors frequently and not persevering with treatments. Last of all – as we have seen throughout this book – melancholy varies wildly from one individual to another, and what might suit one sufferer can cause irreparable damage to another. Doctors must treat their melancholic patients sensitively, and make sure that the non-naturals are finely tuned to each person's circumstances, age, and constitution.

The old proverb that 'prevention is better than cure', recorded by the Dutch scholar Erasmus in the early sixteenth century (though with its origins in antiquity), is fundamental to Renaissance medical approaches to the non-naturals. The most popular English medical textbooks from this period were aimed at lay people rather than specialists and take the form of regimens: advice manuals on how to stay healthy and stave off illness by keeping the non-naturals well-balanced. Books such as

Thomas Moulton's *This is the Mirror or Glass of Health* (1531), Thomas Elyot's *The Castle of Health* (1539), and William Bullein's *The Government of Health* (1558) were endlessly reprinted and expanded, capturing the market for short works instructing readers in how to stay well.[1]

The most influential of them of all is the medieval 'Salernitan Regimen of Health' (*Regimen sanitatis Salernitanum*), which is also perhaps the most unusual of medical texts: it is written entirely in verse, designed to make the advice easy both to digest and to remember. Its approach to prevention of illness is based on regulating the non-naturals. Sir John Harington's English translation sums them up neatly:

Drink not much wine, sup light, and soon arise,
When meat is gone long sitting breedeth smart:
And after noon still waking keep your eyes,
When moved you find yourself to *Nature's Need*
Forbear them not, for that much danger breeds,
Use three Physicians still, first Doctor *Quiet*,
Next Doctor *Merry-man*, and Doctor *Diet*.[2]

By following this advice to the letter, a reader might manage to avoid other, more expensive forms of doctor – and keep a healthy daily routine and humoral balance.

For those who are especially prone to black bile or adust (corrupt) humours, regulating the non-naturals can prevent their humoral imbalances from becoming too severe – and Burton notes that in almost every consultation for melancholy, physicians discover a problem with the non-naturals among its origins. The Italian physician Francesco Frigemelica (1491–1559) treated a soldier for this illness and found that he had disorders in all six of the non-naturals, 'which were the outward causes, from which came those inward obstructions' (i.217). That word 'obstructions' is an important one because (as we have already seen) therapy involving the non-naturals characteristically aims to restore healthy humoral flow and break up blockage.

Some pieces of advice concerning the non-naturals are easier to take than others. Stopping eating a favourite food or going to bed earlier might be challenging, but fairly straightforward to achieve. By contrast, the 'rectification of air' (ii.61) is much more complicated: those who live in damp, marshy areas are more prone to corrupt humours than those who live in a place with clean, dry air, but few would be wealthy enough to act on the advice given by the physician Giulio Cesare Chiodini (Claudinus, d. 1618) to the Polish nobleman troubled with melancholy, to 'dwell in a house inclining to the east, and by all means to provide the air be clear and sweet' (ii.64–5). They might at least be comforted to know that living in a house with a moat is considered unwholesome.

The great problem with melancholy is that it weakens willpower. Those who succumb to the disease are influenced by their corrupted imaginations and are not always able to overcome false beliefs and make rational decisions, or stick to them. Following rules and strict routines may be impossible. Melancholics may be beyond preventative advice, but they may still try and alter entrenched and unhealthy habits. Robert Burton's writing on the non-naturals draws attention to the effects of outside environment and daily routines, of big things and small. A melancholic patient might need a clyster; then again, she might simply benefit from opening a window.

Diet

Never invite a melancholic to dinner: that, at least, might be the conclusion we reach after reading Burton's lengthy discussion of how bad diet can be a cause of melancholy (i.216–33). His list of foods and drinks which trigger or exacerbate melancholy, and which he tells sufferers to avoid, is a very long one – so long that it almost seems like a joke, for there seems little left that one safely can eat. It is not just a matter of what kinds of food and drink a melancholic should or should not have, but also how much, how they are prepared, how often they should be consumed, and at what times of day or night. Renaissance dietary regulation is an elaborate art, designed to be precisely attuned to individuals. Of all the non-naturals, diet is the factor which is most easily varied – at least for those who can afford to choose what they eat – and which can make an immediate impact on a patient, for good or ill.

Not only do certain foods cause melancholy, but several are instrinsically melancholy in their properties: most famously hare (Figure 7.1). The animal is a symbol of the disease because it is solitary and timid in its habits; Burton records that the Egyptians used it as a hieroglyphic character for a melancholic (i.396). One of Aesop's fables also suggests their propensity to grief of mind: it is recorded of 'the hares, that with a general consent they went to drown themselves, out of a feeling of their misery; but when thcy saw a company of frogs more fearful than they were, they began to take courage and comfort again' (ii.131). The living characteristics of the animal are transmitted into its qualities as food, making it

FIGURE 7.1 *Hare (Lepus europaeus).* Anselmus Boëtius de Boodt (1596–1610).

a black meat, melancholy, and hard of digestion; it breeds *incubus*, often eaten, and causeth fearful dreams, so doth all venison, and is condemned by a jury of physicians. Mizaldus and some others say that hare is a merry meat, and that it will make one fair, as Martial's epigram testifies to Gellia; but this is *per accidens* [by accident], because of the good sport it makes, merry company and good discourse that is commonly at the eating of it, and not otherwise to be understood. (i.218)

The meat's dark colour is an indicator that it breeds black bile (the same applies to other dark meats including game and even beef). It is difficult to digest and causes 'incubus', a word for a demon that troubles people in their sleep but which in Burton's usage here probably means a sense of heaviness on the stomach associated with nightmares and restlessness at night; the condition was also known as being 'witch-ridden'.[3]

The *Anatomy*'s desciption of hare's meat illustrates the fact that medieval and Renaissance medical authorities are by no means in agreement on which foods are good for melancholics and which should be avoided. Burton, the meticulous cataloguer, collects everything that his many medical sources say could possibly be detrimental. Beef, pork, goat, venison, milk, butter, cheese, pigeons, duck, fish, cucumbers, melons, cabbage, herbs and salads, fruits, root vegetables, pulses, spices, honey, sugar, oat bread and rye bread are all condemned by one medical writer or another for their propensity to breed melancholy humours (i.217–23). Burton's list of every medical opinion reads rather like someone has collected every foodstuff reported as being bad for the health in the popular press: the cumulative effect is overwhelming.

Nonetheless, Burton is careful to document what different writers have said rather than to put a blanket prohibition on all the foods they mention. He balances authorities against one another, noting where one writer disagrees with another or where the common view is challenged. Whether this makes the melancholic's task of choosing the right foods any easier is questionable.

Fish is a case in point. 'Rhasis, and Magninus discommend all fish, and say they breed viscosities, slimy nutriment, little and humorous nourishment', notes Burton, but other writers reject only certain freshwater fish like eels, tench, and lamprey which have a muddy taste. Paulus Jovius, on the other hand, 'highly magnifies' lampreys and says that 'none speak against them but *inepti* [fools] and *scrupulosi*, some scrupulous persons'. Meanwhile Gomesius 'doth immoderately extol sea fish, which others as much vilify'; 'Tim. Bright excepts lobster and crab. Massaria commends salmon, which Bruerinus contradicts … Magninus rejects conger, sturgeon, turbot, mackerel, skate' (i.219–20). For every writer who praises the health-giving properties of a particular fish, Burton can find another who disagrees. He devotes 250 words to weighing up the merits and disadvantages of eating carp and gives references to eleven Latin sources that may be consulted on both sides of the debate, before concluding that it all depends what kind of pool the carp is fished from and whether the water is muddy or sweet: hardly advice that would help anyone deciding what they want for dinner.

Though this might give the impression that Renaissance dietary advice is hopelessly muddled – or muddling – there are, however, some positive principles which one can follow to moderate or expel melancholy. Renaissance physicians prescribe foods that are moist, lean, easy to digest and of light colour – chicken is on the menu; swan is not – while anything that causes wind is best avoided. Hence cabbage is dangerous while lettuce is safe to eat. The same applies to drink: white wine is better than red, lighter beer is better than dark ale. Thick and heavy drinks such as muscatel, malmsey, and the sweet wine known as 'brown bastard' should not be drunk (i.223). Food that is boiled is better than anything fried or roasted; the German physician Johann Crato (1519–85) allows the last 'if the burned and scorched superficies, the brown we call it, be pared off' (ii.22). This guidance works on the principle that anything which is dark-coloured and hard to digest will stimulate melancholy.

The type of food and how it is is prepared make a difference to the melancholic constitution. So too does the quantity: Renaissance manuals of health warn of the perils of excessive consumption, not only on the body but on the mind. In particular, drunkenness has well-attested effects on the imagination. Burton records the story of a group of young men from Agrigento in Sicily who, after having 'freely taken their liquor' in a tavern, became so crazed in their imaginations that they became convinced they were in a ship during a storm. Terrified of shipwreck, they threw all the goods in the house out of the windows and into the street, 'or into the sea, as they supposed'. When they were brought before the town magistrate to account for their misdeeds, one of them knelt down and beseeched the sea gods to be merciful, in return for which they vowed to build an altar when they finally reached land. 'The magistrate could not sufficiently laugh at this their madness, bid them sleep it out, and so went his ways' (i.372–3).

While too much strong drink damages our physical and mental faculties, so does excessive and over-rich food. The classic Galenic image of the body is as a lamp burning oil, and when someone eats too much, 'as a lamp is choked with a multitude of oil, or a little fire with overmuch wood quite extinguished, so is the natural heat with immoderate eating strangled in the body' (i.226). Short intervals between meals are also damaging for the health, and Burton turns to his own experience when he observes that Oxford colleges are in the bad habit of serving meals too often – scarcely five hours apart – when seven is the optimum for health. Weighing up his sources, he suggests that it is better to eat a large meal in the evening than in the middle of the day.

As for the size of portions, Burton's advice from his medical sources is to eat only when you feel hungry and to chew everything thoroughly, since melancholics tend to have good appetites but suffer from poor digestion (ii.26–7). Crato provides further wisdom on the subject of what order in which to eat dishes: he recommends that we should eat 'liquid things first, broths, fish, and such meats as are sooner corrupted in the stomach; harder meats of digestion must come last' (ii.28). It is intriguing to find rules about the order of menus – associated with French *haute cuisine* – in the casebooks of a sixteenth-century German doctor.

At the other extreme from gluttony and inebriation are those who take too much care over maintaining a strict diet. These people are 'over-precise, cockney-like, and curious in their observations of meats, times' – a 'cockney' in this context meaning a person who is fastidious and pampered.[4] Dietary regulation can become an obsessive habit for some melancholics who may start to measure out their food, 'just so many ounces at dinner … a diet-drink in the morning, cock-broth, china-broth, at dinner … the merry-thought [wishbone] of a hen, etc.' (i.230). Burton suggests that it is absurd for anyone to eat an invalid's diet when they are strong enough to eat ordinary food, and he reserves particular scorn for those who fast immoderately for religious reasons and become delusional as a result.

When all these complex dietary rules are taken into account, Burton makes an important exception, one that is very much in the spirit of treatments for melancholy. He calls this Cardan's rule (after the Italian physician Cardano):

> to keep that we are accustomed unto, though it be naught; and to follow our disposition and appetite in some things is not amiss; to eat sometimes of a dish that is hurtful, if we have an extraordinary liking to it. Alexander Severus loved hares and apples above all other meats, as Lampridius relates in his life; one pope pork, another peacock, etc.; what harm came of it? I conclude, our own experience is the best physician; that diet which is most propitious to one is often pernicious to another; such is the variety of palates, humours, and temperatures, let every man observe and be a law unto himself. (ii.29)

The advice reveals the writer at his most gently humane, but also, seemingly, at his most paradoxical. Why bother with rules if we can be dietary laws unto ourselves? Yet Burton's approach is building on ancient authority here, for it was the Father of Medicine, Hippocrates himself, who taught that 'such things as we have been long accustomed to, though they be evil in their own nature, yet they are less offensive' (i.230) to the person who is used to them than to anyone else.

This applies to the idiosyncrasies of individuals (such as the pope who liked peacocks) and also to the dietary habits of entire regions and nations – a subject in which Burton shows great interest. For example, medical writers say that cider causes bad wind and can breed melancholy, yet in the great cider regions of Europe – Herefordshire, Gloucestershire, and Worcestershire in England; Normandy in France; Guipúscoa in Spain – the residents happily drink it with no sign of harm to themselves. Local custom may be more important than universal rules, and even something unwholesome might have its benefits once in a while. Nonetheless, while he acknowledges that it is hard to keep to a strict diet ('as good be buried', ii.29), a little self-denial is better than the alternative.

Retention and Evacuation

The effects of diet do not stop with consumption. Once food has been digested, its waste material must be excreted. How the body gets rid – or fails to get rid – of excess matter is another of the non-naturals which can be manipulated for healing purposes, as the case of the merchant at Nördlingen Fair has shown. Both obstruction and excessive flow can be damaging; as we have already seen in Chapter 5, too little sex holds in and corrupts vital fluids, whereas too much 'evacuation' dries and cools the body and also imperils the health. It follows that physical therapy for melancholy may involve either restoring blocked flow – prescribing sex or a clyster – or stopping immoderate excretion, such as diarrhoea or a burst haemorrhoid.

The methods Renaissance physicians used for relieving patients' corrupt humours are as well known as they might appear drastic to us: purging through enemas and vomits, lancing boils, letting blood. We will hear more about surgical cures in the next chapter. Yet Burton is wary of violent therapies of any kind because melancholic patients are often delicate of constitution. The physical strength of the individual patient makes a difference to what kinds of purgative treatments might be safe to prescribe: though a single enema cured the melancholy of the delusional merchant, too frequent treatments could weaken someone beyond safe limits. What 'too frequent' means is debatable, and several sources recommend ensuring that the patient has daily bowel movements by nature or art: 'art' in this case meaning suppositories, prunes, or turpentine enemas (ii.30).

Gentler treatments are a better course of action in most cases and, among them, therapeutic baths rank highly as treatments for melancholy. Though full immersion in a bath was not a frequent practice in Renaissance England and surface washing was far more common, medical writers acknowledge that the practice can be beneficial when it is done judiciously.[5] First of all, feeling fresh and clean is a good form of therapy for the troubled in mind: washing one's hands and face, putting on clean clothes, and changing bedsheets are all means to lift a patient's dejected spirits. Secondly, baths moisten and warm the body, counteracting the natural properties of black bile. And thirdly, they can be fragranced with healing herbs like camomile, violets, or borage – though if this seems too pleasant a remedy, one recipe for treating melancholy involves boiling a ram's head and steeping it in the waters; Burton does not specify whether the patient should remove the ram's head before getting in the bath (ii.30–1).

In the seventeenth century, the ruins of ancient baths could still be found across England amongst 'those parietines and rubbish of old Roman towns' (ii.31; 'parietines' means 'fallen walls' – a word unique to Burton).[6] The sheer number of bathhouses found in the ruins of private homes and urban spaces – chief among them Bath – provided evidence to Burton and his contemporaries of how important bathing was in Roman culture. Many of the techniques and habits taken from both ancient Roman and modern Turkish bathing rituals were of interest to European physicians for therapeutic purposes, including the use of sweat rooms, and the application of ointments to be lathered on the skin and scraped off.

While mineral spas were widespread across Renaissance Europe, physicians were not unanimous in praise of them. Traces of iron, alum, and sulphur were thought to be beneficial for hypochondriacal or windy melancholy, but nonetheless the temperature of the water might be damaging for an overheated liver. Bodily temperament is everything: for those with cold diseases (like an excess of black bile), baths like the ones found in Baden or Bath itself are commendable, but Burton warns that they may be damaging for anyone 'choleric, hot and dry, and all infirmities proceeding of choler, inflamations of the spleen and liver' (ii.32).

Exercise

While hot water might expel gross humours through the skin, an easier and more freely available means of achieving the same is through exercise. The medical guidance for this is quite specific. Galen stresses that exercise should be done 'till the body be ready to sweat' (ii.71) but no more strenuously. In a linguistically pleasing Latin adage, the goal we should aim for is '*ad ruborem*' (towards reddening) rather than '*ad sudorem*' (towards sweating), otherwise the risk of the body drying out may be too great.

Exercise should always be done before a meal, preferably on an empty stomach. The sixteenth-century physician Prospero Calani Centurione (Calenus) prescribes it to his patient as part of a morning routine, after he has 'done his ordinary needs, rubbed his body, washed his hands and face, combed his head and gargarized [gargled]' (ii.71). Another man of the same profession, Leonhard Fuchs (Fuchsius, 1501–66), warns of the dangers of not heeding this advice, claiming that German schoolboys are prone to scabies because they only run around and play straight after a meal, which builds up crude humours within them.

Far more risky than too much exercise is not enough. Idleness is both a cause and a symptom of melancholy, and every effort should be taken to avoid it. It is 'the badge of gentry', as Burton puts it: the wealthy do not need to do an honest's day's labour and can afford to spend their time in leisure. Laziness incurs Burton's strong censure, prompting him towards homiletic mode. It is:

> the bane of body and mind, the nurse of naughtiness, step-mother of discipline, the chief author of all mischief, one of the seven deadly sins, and a sole cause of this and many other maladies, the devil's cushion, as Gualter calls it, his pillow, and chief reposal. (i.242)

The habit breeds like an algal bloom. In Seneca's words, 'as in a standing pool, worms and filthy creepers increase … so do evil and corrupt thoughts in an idle person'. One of Burton's examples is Achilles in Homer's *Iliad* after he has refused to go into battle at the siege of Troy, 'eating of his own heart in his idleness, because he might not fight'. A lack of occupation and stimulation corrupts even the greatest men, and while Burton is sympathetic to the difficulties of melancholics, his tone is unmistakably sharp: neglecting physical exercise is 'nothing but a benumbing laziness' (i.242–3).

What kinds of exercise are the best for expelling melancholy? The physical forms of exercise that Renaissance medical writers recommend are of the kind we might now classify as of moderate intensity. Some are more vigorous, such as ball games, 'quoits, pitching bars, hurling, wrestling, leaping, running, fencing, mustering, swimming, wasters, foils, football … and many such, which are the common recreations of the country folks', as well as more socially elite occupations such as jousting tournaments and horse races (ii.74). Burton's favoured forms of exertion, however, are those that 'recreate Body and Mind' together.

The typical pursuits of the English nobility – hawking and hunting – are praised for being stimulating activities, but all the more so is fishing, 'a kind of hunting by water'. It is an ideal occupation for the melancholic because it is spent outside in pleasant surroundings, involves mental attention, and breeds tranquility. Though Plutarch speaks against it as a filthy, base occupation, Burton's response to this criticism is beautiful:

> But he that shall consider the variety of baits for all seasons, and pretty devices which our anglers have invented, peculiar lines, false flies, several sleights, etc. will say that it deserves like commendation, requires as much study and perspicacity as the rest, and is to be preferred before many of them. Because hawking and hunting are very laborious, much riding, and many dangers accompany them; but this is still and quiet: and if so be the angler catch no fish, yet he hath a wholesome walk to the brookside, pleasant shade by the sweet silver streams; he hath good air, and sweet smells of fine fresh meadow flowers, he hears the melodious harmony of birds, he sees the swans, herons, ducks, water-hens, coots, etc., and many other fowl, with their brood, which he thinketh better than the noise of hounds, or blast of horns, and all the sport that they can make. (ii.73–4)

Burton lived close to the River Thames in Oxford, and the gentle pleasures still to be found at the waterside there are ones he presumably knew well. A few decades after the first publication of the *Anatomy*, Izaak Walton would dedicate a whole book to the pleasures of fishing, *The Compleat Angler, Or The Contemplative Man's Recreation* (1653) and make the case that not only is it a noble and ancient activity, but also one that brings you closer to God; after all, he points out, Jesus' closest friends and disciples were all fishermen.[7]

The restorative effects of taking moderate exercise in 'pleasant and delightsome places', as André du Laurens puts it, are well attested in Renaissance medical literature.[8] But Burton takes this one step further, enriching his description with overflowing details:

> To walk amongst orchards, gardens, bowers, mounts, and arbours, artificial wildernesses, green thickets, arches, groves, lawns, rivulets, fountains, and such-like pleasant places, like that Antiochian Daphne, brooks, pools, fishponds, between wood and water, in a fair meadow, by a river-side ... to disport in some pleasant plain, park, run up a steep hill sometimes, or sit in a shady seat, must needs be a delectable recreation. (ii.74–5)

This is one of the many examples where Burton keeps on expanding his text as he revises it over the years. Between the first edition of the *Anatomy* (1621) and the third (1628) he adds 'mounts', 'lawns', 'rivulets', 'fountains', 'brooks', and a 'park' to this description, making it all the more pastoral and idyllic.[9] The Antiochian Daphne is an addition too: the grove of the nymph Daphne was a place of sanctuary celebrated by classical writers for its beauty, its abundant springs and woods.

Of course, the grove at Antioch was long gone by the seventeenth century. That Burton includes it in his description of the outside world reminds us that this scholar's own recreations were born in the library. Along with his own collection of over 1,700 books, he had the Bodleian Library (Figure 7.2) and that of his own college at his disposal. Reading books is an activity that he warmly recommends to melancholics: 'amongst those exercises or recreations of the mind within doors, there is none so general, so aptly to be applied to all sorts of men, so fit and proper to expel idleness and melancholy, as that of study' (ii.86). Whether we acquire knowledge about the ancient world, look at the great maps and atlases of Ortelius and Mercator, learn languages, study architecture, botany, and zoology, or learn poetry off by heart, all of these will bring pleasure, refreshment, and occupation

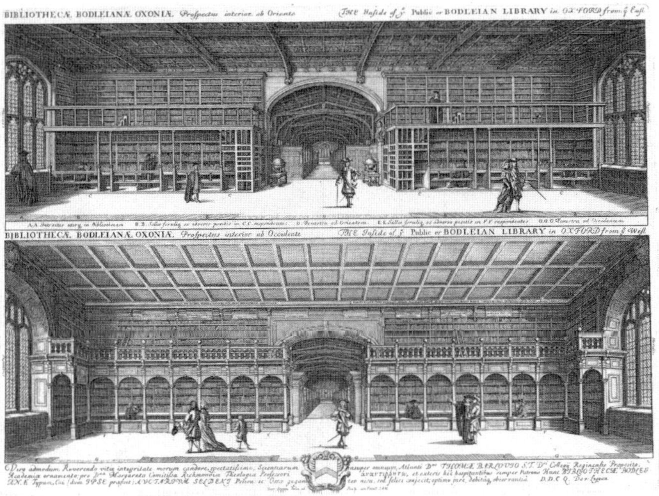

FIGURE 7.2 Interior of the Bodleian Library in Oxford. David Loggan (1675).

to our troubled minds. To read is to seek solace, and – as the physician Cardano puts it – libraries are 'the physic of the soul' (ii.93).

Burton's enthusiastic endorsement of study's health-giving properties is nonetheless surprising, since most other Renaissance medical writers actively discourage melancholics from undertaking intellectual activity. Timothy Bright, for instance, advises sufferers to 'above all, abandon working of your brain with study'; even Burton himself – the lifelong Oxford scholar – chronicles the many miseries of scholars in his description of the causes of melancholy.[10] Burton bids caution in not overtiring oneself or becoming addicted to books. Once again, causes, symptoms, and cures bleed into one another, as, for those whose melancholy is rooted in too much study, more of the same will hardly be curative and only 'adds fuel to the fire'. For everyone else who is mentally afflicted, though, he is unequivocal that it does them good: by providing distraction and mental nourishment, reading diverts their harmful 'continual meditations' (ii.92–3) and calms the mind.

The non-naturals are a mainstay of short- and long-term therapy. They demand daily attention: neglect one even for a short while and the effects may be severe and unexpected (as the merchant at Nördlingen discovered); establish a careful routine and the disease might be gradually overcome. While advice about hygiene might seem broad-brushed, for melancholics it is especially important to take care of personal habits which can easily become engrained and obsessive if they are uncontrolled. Part of the responsibility lies upon the individual sufferer, to exercise, take the air, eat well, keep clean; but in cases of melancholy, even basic bodily functions may need the intervention of others. In the next chapter, we shall see the form that some of these interventions took in the sixteenth and seventeenth centuries, as we enter the melancholy pharmacopoeia.

8

Medicine and Surgery

"Many things" (saith Penottus) "are written in our books, which seem to the reader to be excellent remedies, but they that make use of them are often deceived, and take for physic poison." I remember in Valleriola's Observations, a story of one John Baptist a Neapolitan, that finding by chance a pamphlet in Italian, written in praise of hellebore, would needs adventure on himself, and took one dram for one scruple, and had not he been sent for, the poor fellow had poisoned himself. From whence he concludes out of Damascenus ... "that, without exquisite knowledge, to work out of books is most dangerous: how unsavoury a thing it is to believe writers, and take upon trust, as this patient perceived by his own peril." I could recite such another example of mine own knowledge, of a friend of mine, that finding a receipt in Brassavola, would needs take hellebore in substance, and try it on his own person; but had not some of his familiars come to visit him by chance, he had by his indiscretion hazarded himself; many such I have observed.

(Burton, *Anatomy*, ii.20)

Burton begins his discussion of the cures of melancholy with a warning. If we read a book like *The Anatomy of Melancholy*, we may be tempted to use its advice not just to regulate the habits of our daily lives – our non-naturals – but also to self-medicate. Instead of finding therapy and relief from sadness, fear, and melancholic delusion, we may instead worsen our conditions. We may even run the risk of accidentally killing ourselves. Scenting our rooms with rose water to calm our troubled minds might be safe and beneficial (ii.66); attempting to purge ourselves with hellebore is certainly not.

Renaissance manuals on melancholy contain cures of two basic types. The first type is the one which we surveyed in the previous chapter and consists of recommended changes to behaviour, the environment around us, and patterns of thought. A melancholic may be advised to get up earlier, to take up a new form of exercise, or to alter diet. But even then, the cure is not necessarily self-led. The sufferer may need someone else to persuade or trick him out of a fixed mental habit, like the man who was convinced he was dead and refused to eat until a skilled physician had his assistant dress up as a corpse lying in a wooden chest next to the patient's bed, and sit up and take refreshments; when the patient asked the man whether dead men ate, the apparent corpse assured him that they did, 'whereupon he did eat likewise and was cured' (ii.115). Even with the non-naturals, the services of a medical practitioner may be needed.

The second type of cure involves medicinal preparations (or 'physic') and surgical interventions, which are the subject of this chapter. The most basic form of them is the 'simple', the treatment consisting of a single active ingredient: a flower or herb such as hellebore, borage, or St John's wort; or a mineral or precious stone such as topaz, emeralds, or antimony. Then there are compounds, prepared from multiple ingredients and typically taken in the form of syrups, wines, pills, or topical ointments. Medicines may be designed to strengthen the body and ward off a disease, or on the other hand to purge the body of its corrupt and excessive humours. Surgical procedures – bloodletting, cauterising wounds, trepanning – are designed to have the same effect. Before we examine these pharmaceutical and surgical treatments, however, we must first look at the dangers of treating melancholy this way, and at the ways in which people accessed medical help in Renaissance England.

Risky Medicine

In writing a book in English directly addressed towards those affected by melancholy, Burton acknowledges that he has widened his readership beyond the learned, such as the medical professionals who would consult Latin textbooks. The enterprise of writing in the language of ordinary speech rather than the universities is potentially hazardous, because it puts into the hands of lay consumers knowledge that they may not use judiciously and with moderation. Reading is no substitute for training. Burton occasionally slips into untranslated Latin for subjects that he wishes to keep from some of his readers (though not all of these are medical: one self-censored passage is about unusual sexual proclivities and starts 'Semiramis equo' ('Semiramis with a horse'), iii.50–2).

Books on melancholy in the vernacular – by Timothy Bright, André du Laurens, and Burton – all come with a health warning. Bright starts his chapter on medicines with a direct admonition:

> my meaning is not to make you a physician, or to give warrant by this my labour to any rashly, and without direction of the learned physician, to adventure practice upon this advice, as the common sort is too venturous to attempt what they read of medicine delivered in their vulgar tongue.

Instead, he continues, his melancholic reader should find out about what drugs are typically prescribed for melancholy and thus gain confidence in the prescriptions given by the learned physician. For the art is a highly skilled one, which demands respect:

> medicine is like a tool and instrument of the sharpest edge, which not wisely guided, nor handled with that cunning which thereto appertaineth, may bring present peril in stead of health, and where it should be a succour, and maintenance of life, for want of art, may work a contrary effect, dangerous, and deadly.[1]

Those who proceed to learn about medicinal treatments must do so with these cautions in mind, and at their own risk.

Burton's warning goes even further. While Bright is worried about those readers who venture to try out what they have read in the 'vulgar tongue' (the vernacular), Burton knows that even highly educated people can do themselves harm. The two stories with which we began this chapter, of unqualified people who nearly poisoned themselves, illustrate this clearly. The first, the Italian John Baptist, was reading a pamphlet in his mother tongue when he appears to have misunderstood the symbols for apothecaries' weights: the abbreviation for a dram (1/8 of an ounce) is ʒ, similar to a scruple (1/24 of an ounce), ℈. Without the lucky intervention of the physician Valleriola, the man would have taken triple the recommended dose. Burton's friend nearly overdosed on the same drug, hellebore, but in this case it was through reading the Italian medical writer Antonio Musa Brassavola. Brassavola's works were not translated into English, and so presumably his friend was reading them in the original Latin. Though he understood which plant was being referred to, he tried to take hellebore in its pure, undiluted form ('in substance') without considering its potential effect on him.

Melancholics put themselves at risk when they self-prescribe, and not just because they might read a recipe incorrectly. The art of medical reading is also about interpreting individual human bodies through the symptoms they display and their humoral predispositions, against the accumulated tradition of learned medicine. As Burton comments:

> That which is conducing to one man, in one case, the same time is opposite to another. An ass and a mule went laden over a brook, the one with salt, the other with wool: the mule's pack was wet by chance, the salt melted, his burden the lighter, and he thereby much eased: he told the ass, who, thinking to speed as well, wet his pack likewise at the next water, but it was much the heavier, he quite tired. So one thing may be good and bad to several parties, upon diverse occasions. (ii.19–20)

A skilled physician can read the signs of a patient and diagnose and prescribe based on the myriad individual variables they have taken into account. An amateur reader of textbooks, by contrast, has none of the experience needed to make these nuanced decisions.

Untrained people such as John Baptist and Burton's anonymous friend were able to get hold of potentially lethal drugs because of the way that medical practice was structured. In Renaissance England, practitioners came in many different forms: from doctors who had trained in medicine at university and were licensed by the Royal College of Physicians, to barber-surgeons and apothecaries, to a wide range of unlicensed lay practitioners including folk healers, clergy, and gentry women (as we will see later, Burton's own mother was one of these last healers). Pharmaceutical ingredients and compounds were sold retail at apothecaries' shops. While patients who could afford the services of a licensed physician would take a prescription to the apothecary to be made up, others might buy prepared medicines without a prescription, or indeed buy single ingredients directly to make up their own recipes at home. Apothecaries were allowed to supply medicines but not to treat people; in practice, though, they sometimes did provide medical advice, especially in areas beyond the major urban centres, where few trained physicians were available.[2]

As well as physicians and apothecaries, there was a wide variety of lay people who offered treatments of one kind or another. Village ministers might provide their parishioners with physical as well as spiritual care; the sick poor might consult wise women and cunning folk; mountebanks or quack doctors travelled from place to place. Though Burton does not describe the whole spectrum of the medical marketplace, he has contemptuous words for those wealthy people who have habitual recourse to pharmaceuticals, 'a few nice idle citizens, surfeiting courtiers, and stall-fed gentlemen lubbers'. He regards them as decadent, self-indulgent, and pampered. As for everyone else, 'the country people use kitchen physic, and common experience tells us that they live freest from all manner of infirmities that make least use of apothecaries' physic' (ii.208).

It is a disconcerting aspect of *The Anatomy of Melancholy* – one of many – that Burton begins his discussion of medicines by denouncing physicians. Upholding the myth that primitive peoples – including the inhabitants of Britain – did not need medicines and were naturally healthy and long-lived, he argues that formal medical practice has only served to make people's health worse. Medical doctors are murderers, he claims, citing the Dutch proverb that 'a new physician must have a new graveyard' (ii.208): their patients would have survived if only they had been left to recover naturally. Medicine is a corrupt, mercenary trade, full of malicious fraudsters and sharp businessmen who would rather get one up on their rivals than heal the sick. Their supposed cures rarely work and they contradict one another's advice; if they do manage to cure a sick person, it is more out of good luck and the patient's confidence rather than genuine skill. There are many diseases – epilepsy, bladder stones, gout – that physicians cannot cure at all (ii.208–11).

This tirade continues for several pages until Burton brings himself up short: 'I will urge these cavilling and contumelious arguments no farther, lest some physician should mistake me, and deny me physic when I am sick' (ii.211). Typically contrary, he goes on to insist that medicine is a 'a divine science': Apollo and Aesculapius were worthily called gods by the Greeks and Romans for having founded it; the scriptures extol it; and misuses of it do not undermine its noble nature. Abrupt changes of direction are nothing new to Burton. His reversals are satirical games holding up a mirror to human nature's contradictions. If his words ridicule and denigrate medicine, they do so because everything earthly is worthy of ridicule and attack; he is Democritus Junior, the laughing philosopher. Doctors are fallible and medicine is an evolving art, not a fixed set of knowledge; it strives imperfectly towards improvement as the secrets of nature gradually reveal themselves to each new age: 'experience teaches us every day many things which our predecessors knew not of' (ii.223). We still have much to learn.

Hellebore

What medicines might a melancholic take to ease this complex condition of body, mind, and soul? There are two basic types of remedy in Renaissance medicine, classified by the way they work on the body. Alteratives strengthen the body, fight off diseases, and correct nature. Purgatives, on the other hand, void the body of excess and bad humours, working either upwards through vomits or downwards through enemas. Alteratives and purgatives can be found in the form of simples (that is, as single ingredients) or compounds and as liquids or solids.

The oldest and most famous remedy for melancholy is hellebore, the flowering evergreen plant with purging properties (Figure 8.1). There are two varieties, black and white, black hellebore being the more commonly used while white hellebore was thought to be far stronger and more toxic. It was used for a wide variety of ailments including vertigo, leprosy, palsy, sciatica, tetanus, and flatulence, and was even used as rat poison, but above all it was associated with treating melancholy, insanity, and delirium.

The story of its discovery comes from Pliny the Elder. A shepherd called Melampus was grazing his goats when he noticed that, after they had eaten some hellebore plants, they purged violently. The daughters of King Proetus of Argos had been struck down with madness.

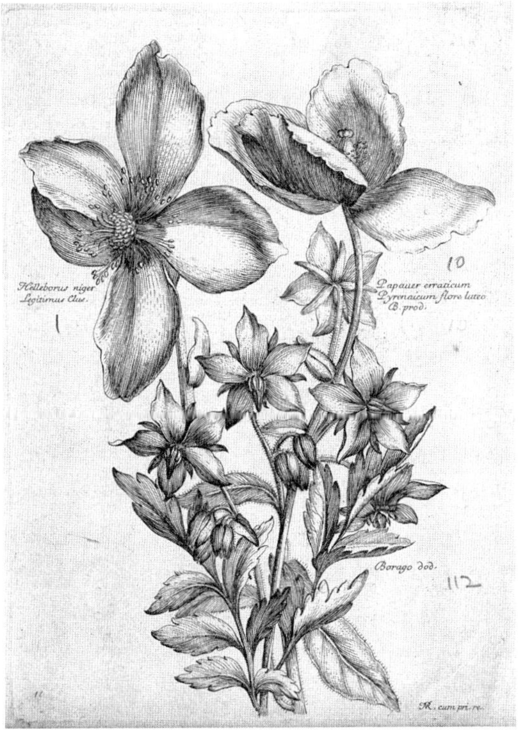

FIGURE 8.1 A Christmas rose (*Helleborus niger*), a poppy (Papaver species), and borage (*Borago officinalis*): flowering stems. Etching by N. Robert (c. 1660), after himself.

Melampus offered to cure them, and did so successfully by giving them the hellebore-tainted milk from his goats. The best hellebore was grown at Anticyra on a peninsula of the Corinthian Gulf; the proverbial saying that someone needed to sail to the Anticyrae was another way of suggesting that they were mad. A similar piece of proverbial wisdom became immortalised on the late sixteenth-century Fool's Cap Map, which depicts the head of a jester whose face is Ortelius' map of the world. The words 'Ô caput elleboro dignum' are written across the top of the jester's hat: 'O head in need of hellebore'; the world itself needs purging of its madness, the saying implies (i.39).[3]

Nonetheless, hellebore was not just used for treating illness. It was also well known in the ancient world as an intellectual sharpener, stimulating wit and literary production. The Sceptic philosopher Carneades, for example, was said to have taken it to help him compose a response to the treatises of Zeno. This last example reminds us of melancholy's dual status as a serious disease and as a marker of genius, in the tradition established by the pseudo-Aristotelian *Problems*.[4]

How was hellebore taken? The active ingredient was found in the plant's root, and several Italian physicians of the sixteenth century used it in this pure form: Gabriello Fallopio (after whom the Fallopian tube is named) did so, as did Brassavola,

> who brags that he was the first that restored it again to its use, and tells a story how he cured one Melatasta, a madman, that was thought to be possessed, in the Duke of Ferrara's court, with one purge of black hellebore in substance: the receipt is there to be seen; his excrements were like ink, he perfectly healed at once. (ii.232)[5]

As was often the case in this period, the acid test of a medicine's effectiveness was its capacity to produce a noticeable effect. The black-bile-ridden excrements of Melatasta would be read as evidence of how well hellebore worked, the colour of the flower corresponding with the humour it expelled.

As we have seen from Burton's story of his friend's near-overdose, hellebore 'in substance' was highly risky and most medical writers rejected it. Instead, they recommended using the root in an infusion or a concoction, where it still retained its effectiveness. In this form, it even had ingenious military uses: Burton repeats a story of the Athenian statesman 'Solon, that, besieging I know not what city, steeped hellebore in a spring of water, which by pipes was conveyed into the middle of the town, and so either poisoned, or else made them so feeble and weak by purging, that they were not able to bear arms' (ii.231). The story is a reminder that, even in diluted form, the plant had highly toxic properties.

While black hellebore purged downward, white hellebore was used for purging upward and was also known as sneezing powder. Widely sold and used in home recipes, it could have violent effects: Burton complains that people take too little heed of the quantity and buy it by the penny's worth, 'as I have heard myself market folks ask for it in an apothecary's shop: but with what success God knows; they smart often for their rash boldness and folly, break a vein, make their eyes ready to start out of their heads, or kill themselves' (ii.227). That a medicine was herbal did not mean that it was gentle in its effects, and Burton – who held the post of clerk of Oxford market for several years and was responsible for checking that the weights and measures used by traders were accurate – carefully directs his reader towards recipes with precise quantities.[6]

Alteratives

Alongside the many substances that purge the body – hellebore being only the chief of many – are those which strengthen and stimulate a patient. Alteratives work within the body, altering inner processes rather than expelling substances out of it. In doing so, they both prevent and cure ailments. Among other properties they can soothe swelling and reduce pain, balancing out humoral imbalances.

Two blue-flowered herbs, borage and bugloss, take pride of place in the melancholic's medicine cabinet. Both can be used in all kinds of forms: 'juice, roots, seeds, flowers, leaves, decoctions, distilled waters, extracts, oils, etc., for such kind of herbs be diversely varied' (ii.215). Bugloss, from the borage family, is a hot and moist plant that promotes cheerfulness, and so it is the ideal medicine to guard against the cold and dry humour of black bile. Burton wonders whether it might be the same as the mythical drug *nepenthe* mentioned in Homer's *Odyssey*, which the Egyptian woman Polydamma gave Helen of Troy to suppress sorrow:

> Then Helen, daughter of Zeus, took other counsel. At once she cast into the wine of which they were drinking a drug to quiet all pain and strife, and bring forgetfulness of every ill. Whoever should drink this down, when it is mingled in the bowl, would not in the course of that day let a tear fall down over his cheeks, no, not though his mother and father should lie there dead, or though before his face men should slay with the sword his brother or dear son and his own eyes behold it.[7]

Burton's reference to Homer reminds us that although his main sources of information are medical texts, the *Anatomy* is also a literary work interested in the realm of the imagination and in poetic accounts of how people have found cheer for themselves. Helen's mysterious ancient remedy comes to stand for that elusive perfect cure-all for melancholy; perhaps it is not even a drug at all, but simply the means of raising the spirits through good company and cheerfulness.

There is a whole panoply of herbal alteratives for melancholic symptoms taken from classical, medieval, and Renaissance sources, and Burton provides lists of medicines with virtues in healing different parts of the body. For the head, aniseed, lavender, bay, rose, rue, sage, marjoram, and peony are effective; for the heart, saffron, basil, rosemary, violets; for the stomach, wormwood, mint, sorrel, purslane; for the liver, agrimony, fennel, endive, liverwort; for the joints, camomile, St John's wort, and cowslips (ii.215). The list goes on for much longer than this small selection, drawing on all the assembled knowledge of English and European botany found in works such as John Gerard's *Herbal* (1597) and the writings of the Swiss naturalist Conrad von Gesner and the German Basilius Besler. Much of this knowledge would go on to inform Nicholas Culpeper's *The English Physician* (1652), that great compendium of English herbs used for preventing and curing sickness, published in the decade after Burton's death.

To read the writings of Burton and his contemporaries on herbal remedies for melancholy is like looking out over a Renaissance botanical garden. Each complaint, symptom, and body part is linked to a set of herbs which, singly or in combination, has special curative properties. Famous botanical gardens in Europe were attached to the major centres of medical learning: Padua in Italy, Leiden in the Netherlands (Figure 8.2), and Montpellier in France. Oxford's reputation for medical training was much lower than these continental cities but Burton's

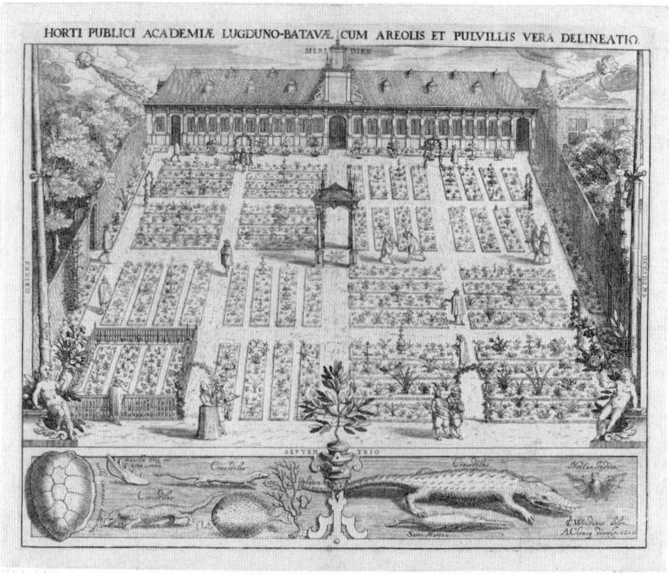

FIGURE 8.2 *Hortus Botanicus of the University of Leiden*. Willem Isaacsz. van Swanenburg, after Jan Cornelisz. van 't Woudt (1610).

home town boasted its own botanic garden, established in the same year that *The Anatomy of Melancholy* was first published, 1621. Burton praises its founder, Henry Danvers, Earl of Danby (who donated not only the land on which it still stands, but also £5,000 to construct it) and its educational benefits. It is a place, he says, 'wherein all exotic plants almost are to be seen, and liberal allowance yearly made for their better maintenance, that young students may be the sooner informed in the knowledge of them'. Though apothecaries rather than physicians handled medicines, Burton urges trainee doctors of medicine to gain practical knowledge of how they work since it is 'as great a shame for a physician not to observe them as for a workman not to know his axe, saw, square' (ii.214).

It was not just plants that offered remedies for the symptoms of melancholy. Along with cordials and ointments, emetics and suppositories, another category of treatments was designed to be worn against the skin. Certain precious stones and minerals were thought to have powerful effects against sorrow and fear. Though not everyone agreed – among them Thomas Erastus, a fierce opponent of the new chemical medicine of Paracelsus in the sixteenth century – Burton finds enough voices in favour. He quotes the approving words of the French pharmacologist Jean de Renou: alongside the fact that these gems 'adorn kings' crowns, grace the fingers, enrich our household stuff, defend us from enchantments, preserve health, cure diseases, they drive away grief, cares, and exhilarate the mind' (ii.218).

The best precious stones for warding off sorrow are garnets, sapphires, and topaz. When hung about the neck, 'they allay anger, grief, diminish madness', while beryl 'represseth vain conceits, evil thoughts, causeth mirth' (ii.218) as well as delighting the mind. Carbuncles and coral drive away fears and troublesome dreams, says the Jesuit Levinus Lemnius; Mercurialis praises emeralds for their virtues 'in pacifying all affections of the mind' (ii.219). The aesthetic qualities of these jewels no doubt play a part in this.

The restorative effects of gemstones and precious metals could also be transmitted by powdering or dissolving them in a potion. *Aurum potabile* – drinkable gold – is the most well known of these: an ancient remedy, gold was championed in the sixteenth century by Paracelsus as a cure of all ills. Burton is attuned to the double meaning of gold's supposedly therapeutic qualities. With an eye for its irony, he quotes Chaucer's *Canterbury Tales*:

For Gold in Physic is a cordial,
Therefore he loved gold in special.[8]

These words are spoken of the physician, playing satirically on the notorious reputation medical doctors had for avarice and wealth gleaned from other people's misfortunes. Gold might have curative effects, but it also provokes other, less noble reactions in humans.

Though critics of Paracelsus fiercely disputed the wisdom of swallowing metal, all writers agreed that pearls were 'very cordial, and most part avail to the exhilaration of the heart' (ii.219). Perhaps one reason for the fact that precious materials were seen as 'exhilarating' is that they were such theatrical remedies, displaying conspicuous consumption quite literally. When Hamlet's uncle Claudius is trying to have his nephew killed during the latter's duel with Laertes, he does so by imitating Cleopatra:

The King shall drink to Hamlet's better breath
And in the cup an union shall he throw
Richer than that which four successive kings
In Denmark's crown have worn.

The Egyptian queen had famously impressed Antony by removing one of her earrings – made from the two largest pearls known in the world – and dropping it in vinegar; she then swallowed the whole draught in front of him. Claudius' action with the 'union' or pearl is a similar show of power and prestige, though with a darker purpose: while he drinks to Hamlet's good health, he also secretly puts poison in Hamlet's cup.[9] Drinking a dissolved pearl delivers an exhilarating 'rush' to the heart which is part of the hedonistic king's flamboyant display;

the same effect on someone sick (and presumably wealthy) would stimulate a weakened heart.

Humbler forms of 'kitchen physic', as Burton calls them, work on a similar principle to jewels. Amulets might be made of herbs – Jean-Baptiste Besard, for instance, recommends St John's wort, gathered on a Friday on a full moon in July and tied in a bunch round the neck – or more unusual substances: Burton approvingly mentions Aetius' remedy of carrying wolf's dung as a cure for colic (ii.250). And in a rare autobiographical moment, he also tells a story from his own family:

> Being in the country in the vacation time not many years since, at Lindley in Leicestershire, my father's house, I first observed this amulet of a spider in a nut-shell lapped in silk, etc., so applied for an ague by my mother; whom, although I knew to have excellent skill in chirurgery, sore eyes, aches, &c., and such experimental medicines, as all the country where she dwelt can witness, to have done many famous and good cures upon divers poor folks, that were otherwise destitute of help: yet, among all other experiments, this methought was most absurd and ridiculous, I could see no warrant for it. *Quid aranea cum febre?* [What has a spider to do with fever?] For what antipathy? till at length, rambling amongst authors (as often I do), I found this very medicine in Dioscorides, approved by Matthiolus, repeated by Alderovandus, *cap. de aranea, lib. de insectis*, I began to have a better opinion of it, and to give more credit to amulets, when I saw it in some parties answer to experience. (ii.250)

The story depicts a meeting-point between learned scholarly medicine and rural practice. Burton's affection for his mother and pride in her skill and charity shine through in this description, but what he dismisses as simply a folk remedy is authorised for him only once he finds a precedent for it in his (male-authored) books. Its logic is at first unclear to him because it does not appear to have properties which counteract the symptoms of fever, and he gives more credit to amulets because he sees their power attested by a string of medical writers from ancient Greece onwards – not by the healing of her patients. Nonetheless, though the story points (perhaps self-deprecatingly) to his bookishness, it also gives an intriguing hint that his interest in medicine might have derived, not from book-learning alone, but also from watching his mother engaged in the practical task of healing the sick.

Surgery

Burton mentions that his mother's medical skills include 'chirugery', or surgery. This is not to imply that Dorothy Burton was performing operations, but rather that her range of therapeutic skills included hands-on interventions for patients with injuries and disease, some of which required instruments. For the treatment of melancholy, such procedures might include shaving the patient's head and rubbing it with cooling ointments, bursting blisters, and applying poultices. The most common surgery was bloodletting (Figure 8.3), and although – as we have seen in Chapter 7 – not all physicians agreed on whether it was a safe procedure to use on melancholics, most argued that it had a place in therapy when performed carefully.

How were Renaissance melancholics bled? The medical texts describe three main techniques. The first is to open a vein by making an incision with a sharp knife.

FIGURE 8.3 A surgeon instructing a younger surgeon how to bleed a male patient's foot; a woman is comforting the patient. Engraving (1586).

The second is to apply cupping glasses: heated cups which are placed on the patient's skin to create a vacuum and draw bad humours out of the body, usually after the skin has been scarified (that is, given a series of scratches and small cuts). The third is to place horse-leeches on parts of the body to suck blood. Burton tells us that this last technique is often used in the treatment of melancholy, being preferred to large incisions because it has a gentler action, and that it is particularly effective when applied to haemorrhoids (ii.235). Further procedures might include cauterising the skin with a hot iron, lancing it, or burning it, but Burton admits that these are extreme. Poultices and mustard plasters are less brutal measures for drawing out corrupt humours, and were more likely to have been used by an informal practitioner like Dorothy Burton.

Not only how a melancholic's blood is drawn out, but also where in the body makes a difference to its healing powers. Those who are afflicted with head melancholy might suffer from high colour in the face, especially when they are afraid or embarrassed, after they have had a large meal, or when they have been drinking. When they blush, 'they think every man observes, takes notice of it', which only exacerbates the condition. For these people – women especially – a physician might recommend bloodletting in the arms or cupping glasses on the shoulders, in order to reduce redness. This works by drawing the blood away from the face, a technique that should be combined with other treatments: perhaps cleansing the face with frog's spawn or anointing it with hare's blood at night, washed off the following morning with water infused with strawberries and cowslips, distilled lemons, or cucumber juice (ii.253–4).

For those patients whose melancholy is all over the body, blood should be let from the arm, usually on the side where there is the most pain, and afterwards the knees or the forehead. But bloodletting should be administered 'to virgins in the ankles, who are melancholy for love matters; so to widows that are much grieved and troubled with sorrows and cares: for bad blood flows in the heart, and so crucifies the mind' (ii.255). The aim is always to draw corrupt blood away from the heart and other organs, where it can do most damage, to the outer extremities. For women whose periods have stopped or who have no sexual experience, encouraging stagnant blood downwards from the womb to the ankles aims to promote healthy flow.

The most extreme form of surgical intervention for melancholy is trepanning, a practice used since the time of Hippocrates and endorsed by a number of Renaissance writers. The sixteenth-century physician Salustio Salviani, for instance, argues that ''tis not amiss to bore the skull with an instrument, to let out the fuliginous vapours', and reports the case of a melancholy man in Rome who had been given all kinds of remedies, none of which worked, until one day he accidentally wounded his head and cracked his skull, which cured his melancholy. Stories of people afflicted with melancholy and madness who recovered after falling from a height or a knock on the head are numerous: the medieval French physician Bernard de Gordon records the story of a melancholic who received a head wound from a sword and who was restored to sanity while the cut stayed open, but succumbed to his dotage again once it healed over. Hence it might be better to keep a hole in the head open if possible: Antonio Guainerio treated a nobleman in Savoy 'by boring alone, "leaving the hole open a month together", by means of which, after two years' melancholy and madness, he was delivered' (ii.242). Such a procedure was a last resort, however, when all other medicines had failed.

Not all medicines needed the careful supervision of a medical practitioner. Common stimulants like tobacco could be beneficial. As he discusses the powers of this substance, Burton shifts sharply from praise to blame in one of his most entertainingly sudden changes of tone:

> Tobacco, divine, rare, superexcellent tobacco, which goes far beyond all the panaceas, potable gold, and philosophers' stones, a sovereign remedy to all diseases. A good vomit, I

confess, a virtuous herb, if it be well qualified, opportunely taken, and medicinally used; but as it is commonly abused by most men, which take it as tinkers do ale, 'tis a plague, a mischief, a violent purger of goods, lands, health, hellish, devilish and damned tobacco, the ruin and overthrow of body and soul. (ii.228)

Perhaps the strength of his reaction demonstrates how far herbal remedies can be used and misused, for good ends and bad. Medical treatment is not a morally neutral territory, and melancholics who are liable to be led by their appetites and imaginations rather than their reasons may be unable to moderate themselves.

One last treatment for melancholy deserves a mention, in the same category as tobacco because it is dangerous if used immoderately. For Burton, however, this remedy has much more to recommend it:

Amongst this number of cordials and alteratives, I do not find a more present remedy, than a cup of wine or strong drink, if it be soberly and opportunely used. It makes a man bold, hardy, courageous, "whetteth the wit", if moderately taken, and (as Plutarch saith, *Symp.* 7. *quaest.* 12.) "it makes those which are otherwise dull, to exhale and evaporate like frankincense," or quicken (Xenophon adds) as oil doth fire. "A famous cordial" Matthiolus *in Dioscoridum*, calls it, "an excellent nutriment to refresh the body, it makes a good colour, a flourishing age, helps concoction, fortifies the stomach, takes away obstructions, provokes urine, drives out excrements, procures sleep, clears the blood, expels wind and cold poisons, attenuates, concocts, dissipates all thick vapours, and fuliginous humours." And that which is all in all to my purpose, it takes away fear and sorrow. (ii.243)

Wine's curative qualities are attested not just in the best medical sources but also in the Bible itself (Psalms 104:15, Proverbs 31:6, 1 Timothy 5:23), Burton the clergyman reminds his readers. It is cheap, common, and works quickly, helping the body's ailments and cheering troubled minds. The great Persian physician Ibn Sina even recommends that melancholics should not just drink, but occasionally allow themselves to get drunk in order to cleanse themselves (ii.245).

As we will see in the final chapter, mirth and good company are excellent cures for a disease characterised by sadness and loneliness. Whereas many of the pharmaceutical and surgical treatments documented in the chapter are unpleasant in their process and in their effects – violent bodily evacuations, bleeding, head wounds – not all cures for melancholy need be disagreeable. A medicine that is pleasant to take and brings with it the benefits of good cheer and sociability has benefits beyond its immediate effects on the human body. Perhaps, after all, that *nepenthe* of Helen of Troy – the mythical ingredient that unfailingly drove away all care and sorrow – was 'naught else but a cup of good wine' (ii.243).

9
Lifting the Spirits

> I write of melancholy, by being busy to avoid melancholy. There is no greater cause of melancholy than idleness, "no better cure than business," as Rhasis holds ... When I first took this task in hand, *et quod ait ille, impellente genio negotium suscepi* [and, as he saith, I undertook the work from some inner impulse], this I aimed at; *vel ut lenirem animum scribendo*, [or] to ease my mind by writing; for I had *gravidum cor, fœdum caput*, a kind of imposthume in my head, which I was very desirous to be unladen of, and could imagine no fitter evacuation than this. Besides, I might not well refrain, for *ubi dolor, ibi digitus*, one must needs scratch where it itches. I was not a little offended with this malady, shall I say my mistress Melancholy, my Egeria, or my *malus genius* [evil genius]? and for that cause, as he that is stung with a scorpion, I would expel *clavum clavo* [a nail with a nail], comfort one sorrow with another, idleness with idleness, *ut ex vipera theriacum* [as an antidote out of a serpent's venom], make an antidote out of that which was the prime cause of my disease.
>
> (Burton, *Anatomy*, i.21)

How do you treat melancholy's bad feelings? Renaissance therapies for 'perturbations of the mind' – the sixth of the Galenic non-naturals – are many and varied. Since melancholy is a disease of the imagination in which the emotions become disturbed, remedies for it must tackle melancholics' emotional states, known in Robert Burton's time as the passions. But how far sufferers can treat themselves, and how far they can be aided by others, is a matter open to question. In this chapter, we will see how self-help, good advice, and emotional regulation work as cures for melancholy – and what their limitations are.

We begin with a case study that is close to home. In the preface to *The Anatomy of Melancholy*, Robert Burton's persona Democritus Junior gives a defence of why he has chosen to write about his subject-matter. His reason might turn our received idea of a medical textbook on its head. He does not write out of a research specialism, nor because he has developed expertise through seeing a large number of cases in practice. Indeed, he is not a physician at all. Instead, he lays claim to far more personal motives. He writes as a form of therapy, to keep himself occupied and to purge his troubled mind. Or is it because he cannot help himself? Artistic creation hovers between symptom and cure: it is an itch that needs scratching.

Though he acknowledges the many years of study that it has taken to put together his *Anatomy*, he also claims another form of authority:

> Concerning myself, I can peradventure affirm with Marius in Sallust, "That which others hear or read of, I felt and practised myself; they get their knowledge by books, I mine by melancholising." *Experto crede Roberto* [believe Robert the expert]. Something I can speak out of experience ... I would help others out of a fellow-feeling; and, as that virtuous lady did of old, "being a leper herself, bestow all her portion to build an hospital for lepers," I will spend my time and knowledge, which are my greatest fortunes, for the common good of all. (i.22)

Even as the Oxford scholar declares an expertise in melancholy born out of hard experience, he does so with a patchwork of quotations from others. His claim that other people get their knowledge out of books whereas his comes from 'melancholising' is itself adapted from a book: Marius in Sallust's *Jugurthine War* is an old soldier who has earned his stripes on the battlefield. Burton wears the literary scars of melancholy and responds to his suffering in the only way he knows how. His intellectual project is both an act of self-help and motivated by a charitable impulse. He wants his readers to get better.

The Anatomy of Melancholy is unique in Renaissance books about melancholy because its impetus for creation stems from the author's own suffering. Or does it? Burton published his book under the pseudonym of Democritus Junior, heir to the laughing philosopher of ancient Greece who, Burton tells us, cut up the carcases of dead animals in order to try and find the seat of madness and melancholy, 'to the intent he might better cure it in himself, and by his writings and observations teach others how to prevent and avoid it' (i.20; Figure 9.1). We can never quite place Burton within his own book. When he writes as 'I', he is also speaking from behind a mask, and we must beware of being too quick to take at face value claims that are all a part of this game-playing. Nonetheless, when he speaks 'out of experience', he lets the mask slip for a moment as he uses his real name for the first and only time: 'Robert the expert'.[1] It seems fair to assume that his claims of suffering from the disease of melancholy are biographically genuine, but that they are intertwined with the literary activity of 'melancholising'. His mistress Melancholy is both an inescapable illness and an artistic muse.

FIGURE 9.1 *Democritus Lost in Meditation.* Salvator Rosa (1662).

Self-Help

How far can melancholics help themselves through reading about their condition? Burton / Democritus Junior says that he has studied books about melancholy 'to do myself good' (i.22), and the possibility of some level of self-treatment is not entirely rejected by medical writers. Burton often addresses his readers directly, imagining that they are seeking a cure, and his English predecessor Timothy Bright claims that *A Treatise of Melancholy* (1586) is written for a supposed friend 'M', who is suffering from the disease. Reading about melancholy is not risk-free, however. In his preface, Burton advises:

> Yet one caution let me give by the way to my present or future reader, who is actually melancholy, that he read not the symptoms or prognostics in this following tract, lest by applying that which he reads to himself, aggravating, appropriating things generally spoken, to his own person (as melancholy men for the most part do) he trouble or hurt himself, and get in conclusion more harm than good. (i.38)

The condition now known as Medical Student Syndrome – in which someone learning about a disease develops symptoms of it – is a classic aspect of melancholy, being typical of the workings of a damaged imagination. Reading about the disease may make those people who are susceptible to it worse rather than better, as they find new symptoms reflected in their bodies or as they amplify minor complaints into serious illnesses. Burton's warning might seem like a joke, though it only applies to certain sections: to read about cures does not carry the same danger.

The very nature of sufferers' minds means that treatment must come, first and foremost, from themselves. Recovery from melancholy hinges on some degree of personal responsibility. If the patient be 'averse, peevish, waspish, give way wholly to his passions, will not seek to be helped or be ruled by his friends, how is it possible he should be cured?' (ii.104). To accept help from others is in itself an act of self-help, and someone who is 'willing at least, gentle, tractable, and desire[s] his own good' puts himself in a better position to be cured, or at least eased in his suffering.

Medical writers highlight certain things that melancholics can concentrate on doing. The first is to resist the beginnings of the disease. This advice applies especially to someone whose humoral disposition tends towards an excess of black bile, and who may tip into habitual disease if it is not carefully checked. If you are aware of a particular preoccupation starting to overtake your mind – whether it is a pleasing one or not – then you should make every effort to resist it in the early stages, before it becomes too strong. The French physician Nicolas le Pois (Piso, 1527–87) recommends a form of shock treatment to change fixed mental habits: when a melancholic succumbs to false fears or strange ideas, he should 'stop upon a sudden, curb himself in' (ii.104), deliberately thinking of something opposite or doing something to distract himself.

The same rule applies to those who are already in the midst of the disease. A sharp change of direction and a self-challenging about delusional ideas may be what is most needed. A philosopher who was bitten by a mad dog contracted the characteristic symptoms of hydrophobia (or rabies), which was seen as associated with melancholy because it caused mental distress and delusion. He became scared of water and believed that he could see a dog continually in front of him. Nonetheless, he forced himself to have a bath, 'and seeing there (as he thought) in the water the picture of a dog, with reason overcame this conceit; *Quid cani cum balneo?* what should a dog do in a bath?' (ii.106). By asserting the power of reason, he managed to conquer his delusional mind. Burton does not mention what became of the philosopher, though presumably his strength of character was no match against all the effects of rabies.

The problem with advice about melancholy is that, to an outsider, it might seem straightforward and easily put into practice. Yet, daringly, Burton allows the sufferer to answer back:

> Yea, but you infer again, *facile consilium damus aliis*, we can easily give counsel to others; every man, as the saying is, can tame a shrew but he that hath her; *si hic esses, aliter sentires*; if you were in our misery, you would find it otherwise, 'tis not so easily performed. We know this to be true; we should moderate ourselves, but we are furiously carried, we cannot make use of such precepts, we are overcome, sick, *male sani*, distempered and habituated to these courses, we can make no resistance; you may as well bid him that is diseased not to feel pain, as a melancholy man not to fear, not to be sad: 'tis within his blood, his brains, his whole temperature, it cannot be removed. (ii.105–6)

It is unusual in a medical manual to find the patient responding to the advice being given. By giving the melancholic a voice, Burton enables mental pain to speak out, and prompts the reader to take it seriously: it is a sickness, just as much as any physical disease, and simply telling a melancholic to stop being sad or fearful will not remove the deep-rooted causes in body as well as mind.

Yet even in speaking from the perspective of the sufferer (perhaps drawing on his own hard-won experience), Burton begins a dialogue. There is no longer a single voice – either that of the physician or of the patient's own mind – that dominates the discourse. Self-help for melancholy is about disrupting a pattern of consuming thoughts, and Burton urges the sufferer not to give in to them: 'rule thyself then with reason, satisfy thyself, accustom thyself, wean thyself from such fond conceits, vain fears, strong imaginations, restless thoughts' (ii.106). Listening to others and putting your own experience into words form part of this process.

If nothing else works, simple practical steps might help. Even if the heart and the imagination will not let go of fixed ideas or overwhelming passions, he suggests that the 'moving faculty' (that is, the power of moving the body) can overrule those urges. If you are afraid of shouting a swearword in the middle of a sermon, you may not be able to stop the 'conceit' or delusional thought, but you can keep your mouth closed. 'In an ague the appetite would drink; sore eyes that itch would be rubbed; but reason saith no, and therefore the moving faculty will not do it' (iii.107). The strength of will that this effort takes, however, is not to be underestimated.

Friendship

Though mild cases can be overcome through small changes in behaviour, Renaissance medical texts agree that even a relatively strong-willed person cannot recover from habitual melancholy without other people's support. The *Aphorisms* of Hippocrates emphasise that cure is built on teamwork. Beginning with the famous statement 'life is short, art long', Hippocrates goes on to stress that 'the Physician exhibit what is essential, and that the patient, attendants, and all which surrounds him, concur therein'.[2] Applied to a case of melancholy, this means that friends and medical practitioners should work together to help a patient who is overcome and unable to resist the passions of the mind.

Simply by speaking to another person, we may find therapy for melancholy. As Burton puts it, 'the best way for ease is to impart our misery to some friend, not to smother it up in our own breast' (ii.107). A friend's good advice, wisdom, and persuasion may work where self-will and the efforts of reason cannot. One explanation for why friendship has a particular curative importance in cases of melancholy is that it combats the loneliness that is a leading cause and symptom. It is fascinating to find Renaissance physicians prescribing company; the Portuguese doctor Rodrigo da Fonseca (d. 1622), for example, insists that patients should not be left either alone or among strangers but rather with those who will love and take care of them.[3] There is an element of keeping melancholics safe from themselves in this instruction, but it is also prompted by the need to prevent sufferers from becoming isolated and preoccupied, and to make sure they are cared for with compassion.

When melancholy is not too engrained, this may be all that is needed. A loved one may hold the key to recovery. The Byzantine physician Alexander of Tralles records the case of a woman who succumbed to melancholy when her husband was away for a long time travelling. She was restored to health at the very first sight of him on his return. In a similar vein, Vittorio Trincavella (1491–1563) treated a Venetian patient who was so troubled with melancholy that he came near to death with sorrow. However, as soon as he heard that his wife had given birth to a son, he recovered instantly (ii.108).

How should people help their melancholic friends? Unsurprisingly, Renaissance medical manuals stress the importance of gentle advice and a kind manner. The aim is to help patients become accustomed to their treatment little by little, and since sufferers are burdened with fear and sorrow, their friends should take care that nothing should be done that might frighten them or cause them grief. Instead, they should try to meet any reasonable requests to make them happy. Cheerful words and distraction are good tactics, as are giving them tasks to occupy them, and writing them letters to encourage and comfort them.

There is one option available if all these tactics fail, though it is not to be used lightly. A tougher form of love may be needed when milder forms of persuasion are not heeded: 'to handle them more roughly, to threaten and chide, saith Altomarus, terrify sometimes, or, as Salvianus will have them, to be lashed and whipped, as we do by a starting horse that is affrighted without a cause' (ii.114). Du Laurens suggests a mixture of praising and shaming the patient, while the Persian physician al-Razi (Rhazes) advocates contrasting approaches: one person should treat the melancholic gently, speaking kind words to them, while the other frightens and chides them, the alternating attitudes being designed to break up the entrenched habits of melancholic thinking.[4]

If shouting at or frightening a melancholic seems unnaturally cruel, one should remember that certain physical forms of treatment operate on a similar principle of 'driving out one nail with another'. Gentle persuasion may be a highly recommended form of treatment, but the Swiss physician Felix Platter also suggests that obdurate melancholy might be cured by pulling out the patient's tooth or castrating him, the latter technique being used since ancient times for the most desperate cases (ii.114). A shock treatment might be needed when all other options have been exhausted, using one emotion – even an unpleasant one – to take the patient's mind off others. While a friend might balk at the idea of deliberately upsetting a melancholic, it is better to give him a sharp fright than to remove his testicles.

Music and Mirth

Cheering melancholics up is a more reliable remedy than terrifying them out of their (damaged) wits. Of all the methods to achieve this, music is universally recommended among Renaissance physicians as one of the most well-attested therapies for easing mental perturbations. Endorsing music's curative properties, they turn to ancient examples to show its power. Thus André du Laurens mentions Clinius, the philosopher who picked up his harp whenever he was overcome with grief or anger, and the psalmist David, who pacified Saul by playing the same instrument (Figure 9.2).[5] And the power of music works not only on people. Recalling the myth of Orpheus, Burton reminds his readers of the many ancient tales of animals and plants – birds, fish, trees – who were charmed by hearing music. 'Harts, hinds, horses, dogs, bears, are exceedingly delighted with it' (ii.117), as are elephants; there is even a story in Cornelius Agrippa of

FIGURE 9.2 *David Plays His Harp before King Saul.* Adriaen Collaert, after Jan van der Straet, 1587–91.

'certain floating islands (if ye will believe it), that after music will dance'.

Why does music work so forcibly on troubled minds? For Timothy Bright, its therapeutic effects stem from the principle of opposites, and from melancholics' susceptibility to sensory stimulation. Since melancholics are easily upset by the evidence of their senses – above all, the things they see and hear, whether real or through the force of their diseased imagination – it stands to reason that the opposite of the source of their distress will heal them. For example, if their fear and sorrow has been stimulated by seeing something alarming, dark, and sinister – a corpse, a devil, a scene on a battlefield – then this effect can be counteracted by surrounding the patient with pleasant and brightly coloured pictures. Likewise, they may be easily distressed by an unpleasant noise such as a scream, but cheerful music will calm and delight them.

Not all music works. Bright recommends music that is lively and simple, unless the melancholic is skilled in music and 'require[s] a deeper harmony'. Meanwhile, anything that is solemn and slow is hurtful, though it will calm someone who is filled with rage or who is inordinately merry; the desired effect on melancholics is 'to allow the spirits, to stir the blood, and to attenuate the humours, which is (if the harmony be wisely applied) effectually wrought by music'.[6] It is striking that Bright sees music working in deeply embodied ways. Not only does the right kind of music cheer someone up, but it thins out thickened, corrupted humours and stirs up the blood – the warm, wet humour that counteracts cold and dry black bile.

Music is therapy for a grieving soul. Drawing on Pythagorean theories of harmony and Platonic philosophy, Renaissance medical writers praise music's healing potency. For Bright, it is a 'magical charm'; for Burton, it is a divine art that 'ravisheth the soul'. Strikingly, Burton also describes it in more forceful terms as 'a roaring-meg against melancholy, to rear and revive the languishing soul; affecting not only the ears, but the very arteries, the vital and animal spirits, it erects the mind, and makes it nimble' (ii.115 16). A 'roaring-meg' is a large cannon, one of the most impressive examples of which, a fifteenth-century cannon also known as 'Mons Meg', was – and still is – at Edinburgh Castle.[7] Whereas other treatments might work gradually and gently, this blasts through the assailing force of melancholy and creates instantaneous effects. Once again, the spiritual effects of music are seen as connected to the inner workings of the human body. It penetrates even to the arteries, through which blood carries the spirits – the fluids that act as messengers between the body and the soul.

Inseparable from music are 'mirth and merry company'. Burton reminds his readers that physicians prescribe all of these things as 'a principal engine, to batter the walls of melancholy' (ii.119–20), being another weapon in the armoury of lifting the spirits. Laughter was considered restorative not just for lifting the spirits but also for reviving the humours. According to Juán Luís Vives, laughter has specific physiological effects: it 'purgeth the blood, confirms health, causeth a fresh, pleasing, and fine colour, prorogues life, whets the wit, makes the body young, lively and fit for any manner of employment' (ii.119). The good medicine of laughter works in a thoroughly embodied way. We have seen how the dark features of a melancholic (in Chapter 2) and the white and green complexion of a love melancholic (in Chapter 5) are signs of their illness; by contrast, the rosy cheeks of someone who laughs are not just signs of good health, but part of the therapy itself as the sanguine humour is stimulated.

Renaissance methods of healing extended well beyond the prescribing of medicines. We find physicians advising melancholics to cheer themselves up with recreations and to find ways of exhilarating their bodies and minds, established as one of the best ways to combat sadness and fear. The authority for this advice comes from medieval Islamic medicine: both al-Razi and Yuhanna ibn Masawaih (Mesue) recommend that patients should be surrounded by sensory delights, given beautiful clothes and furnishings in their rooms, entertained with jests, sports, lively company, music, and even given a cup of drink (ii.120).

There is, of course, a rub. Unless carefully administered, the spirit-lifting properties of music and merriness can cause as many problems as they cure. For a love melancholic, for instance, music may only indulge his frivolities and make him think of nothing else but 'how to make jigs, sonnets, madrigals, in commendation of his mistress'; the writing of romantic poetry should be prevented at all costs. And since melancholics have a tendency to become preoccupied with one thing, a tune may catch their attention so strongly that 'the sound of those jigs and hornpipes will not be removed out of the ears a week after'. It can also provoke strong emotion – 'music makes some men mad as a tiger' (ii.118, 119) – inflaming the mind to dangerous levels.

The same holds true of mirth and merry company. A serious-minded scholar may be healed by playing a game or hearing a good joke, but a sanguine melancholic can tip into mania and laugh for hours or even days. Many people are unable to restrain their merry behaviour and end up whiling away their hours in taverns and brothels, leading to drastic consequences:

> They drown their wits, seethe their brains in ale, consume their fortunes, lose their time, weaken their temperatures, contract filthy diseases, rheums, dropsies, calentures [burning fevers], tremor, get swollen jugulars, pimpled red faces, sore eyes, etc.; heat their livers, alter their complexions, spoil their stomachs, overthrow their bodies; for drink drowns more than the sea and all the rivers that fall into it (mere funges [fungi; fools] and casks), confound their souls, suppress reason, go

from Scylla to Charybdis, and use that which is a help to their undoing. (ii.125)

As ever with melancholy, moderation is the key to restoring healthy balance. But how to work out what is moderate behaviour, when the melancholic imagination has no sense of proportion? Even Burton's list gets beyond itself, as each dire consequence leads to another, and another. His rhetoric tends towards an excess that seems analogous to the experience of drinking that he describes. Melancholy is a disease of extremes, and it is all too easy to go from one to the other, from Scylla to Charybdis – even in the pursuit of good health.

Healing Words

There is one further means of curing a troubled mind, and that is through the consolatory power of words themselves. They may provide the only remedy that is needed, but in order to benefit, the melancholic must first be prepared to undertake a kind of mental and ethical training regime. She may need to regulate her behaviour, learn new ways of handling troubling thoughts, and prepare for difficulties ahead. Burton likens this work of emotional moderation and discipline to a sea voyage. To deal with strong emotions,

> there is no better remedy than as mariners when they go to sea provide all things necessary to resist a tempest, to furnish ourselves with philosophical and divine precepts, other men's examples … to balance our hearts with love, charity, meekness, patience, and counterpoise those irregular motions of envy, livor, spleen, hatred, with their opposite virtues. (ii.186)

While many Renaissance medical manuals acknowledge the need for good advice as therapy for the mentally troubled, a few go further, themselves providing ethical and spiritual guidance for the distressed and grieved.

The Anatomy of Melancholy goes further still. Burton's 'Consolatory Digression, containing the Remedies of all manner of Discontents' (ii.126), is a gathering of 'remedies and comfortable speeches' from rhetoricians and moral philosophers, priests and theological writers, from ancient Greece through to his own contemporaries. Acknowledging that advice does not always work, he nonetheless hopes that it will do some good, and he reminds his afflicted readers that he is one of them: 'if it be not for thy ease, it may be for mine own; so Tully, Cardan, and Boethius wrote *de consol[atione]* as well to help themselves as others' (ii.127). He frames his writing as a form of self-help which he extends to others, following the examples of Cicero (Tully) and Girolamo Cardano, along with Boethius' *Consolation of Philosophy*.

Burton's own consolatory writing is directed towards different groups: those who are grieving the loss of friends or family members; those who are poor or have suffered calamities; people in the grip of envy, hatred, ambition, or shame; the exiled and imprisoned. Each set of experiences and feelings has comforts balanced against it, often drawing on classical moral philosophy: Aristotelian temperance and moderation, Stoical attention to interior virtue instead of external circumstances. Burton stresses that the cause of discontent is 'not in the matter itself, but in our mind, as we moderate our passions and esteem of things' and that true peace is found in patience and a quiet mind (ii.170) rather than in wealth or status.

Yet, all through the 'Consolatory Digression', the voices of sufferers break in. The poor speak back: 'but no man hears us, we are most miserably dejected, the scum of the world ... we can get no relief, no comfort, no succour ... no man living can express the anguish and bitterness of our souls, but we that endure it' (ii.163). Their voices unsettle the simple rhetoric of soothing and consolation, setting up a challenge to well-worn pieces of advice and wisdom. It is as if Burton is stepping from one side of the room to the other, playing both sides of a debate. On one side, he is the counsellor, physician, or caring friend; on the other, he is the sufferer tormented by adversity or trapped inside the prison of his own mental torment.

These moments add a touch of sharp realism, undercutting if they do not undermine generalised pieties. Burton even draws attention to the ridiculousness of proverbial wisdom when he gathers together fifty well-known sayings and lists them all at once: 'Be not idle. Look before you leap. Beware of Had I wist ... Hear much, speak little.' He ends with the advice that if you want more, you should look in the classics or, 'for defect, consult with cheese-trenchers and painted cloths' (ii.205, 206) – a Renaissance equivalent, perhaps, to looking for life advice on a motivational poster or an internet meme. His attempts to 'appease passions or quiet the mind' (ii.189) through consolatory sayings appear to be genuine, but he acknowledges that they sometimes fall short. For Burton, words are far from useless in the face of mental suffering, but they should not be used to erase or deny its reality.

One last consolation falls under Burton's gaze, and that is the consolation against melancholy itself. Beginning with Seneca's idea that everyone 'thinks his own burden the heaviest', he acknowledges that melancholics have many causes of misery but are also the patients who complain the most. Yet, weighed up against other conditions, melancholy has some points in its favour. Firstly, 'it is not catching', and is not repulsive to others (unlike, for instance, the pox): at least melancholics do not smell bad. Secondly, their habits are usually antisocial and so they tend not to disrupt other people's lives, while fear and sorrow restrain them from wild living and dissolute behaviour. Finally, melancholy allows sufferers to be contemplative, reflecting on the fleeting nature of all earthly existence. But if they are foolish and dote, perhaps they may even find happiness in their state of simplicity: 'entire idiots do best', Burton claims (ii.207).

While Burton repeatedly offers the hope that the mentally afflicted can get better, his final consolation against melancholy is the surprising reflection that happiness is not everything. To expect to be happy always is unrealistic: even the greatest moral philosophers were not content all the time. Early on in the *Anatomy*, he reminds his reader that life is bittersweet, 'a mixed passion, and like a chequer-table'. We must learn to suffer affliction, because ''tis most absurd and ridiculous for any mortal man to look for a perpetual tenor of happiness in his life' (i.144–5). Burton looks to the promise of heaven for perfect happiness, and so perhaps a melancholic existence is the best response to the tribulations of earthly life. If others pity us, that is better than their envying us; and perhaps, as some hold, it is 'better to be miserable than happy: of two extremes it is the best' (ii.207).

The Rock of Melancholy

And what of Burton himself? The author who 'was fatally driven upon this rock of melancholy' (i.35) gives no hints of recovery in any of the editions of *The Anatomy of Melancholy*. Although their veracity is doubtful, several posthumous anecdotes suggest that his melancholy grew worse rather than better. In the early eighteenth century, Bishop White Kennett repeated a rumour that

> nothing at last could make him laugh, but going down to the bridge-foot in *Oxford*, and hearing the barge-men scold and storm and swear at one another at which he would set his hands to his sides, and laugh most profusely. Yet in his college and chamber so mute and mopish that he was suspected to be *Felo de se*.[8]

That rumour of suicide (*felo de se*) probably came from the short biography by Anthony Wood, who repeated the gossip that Burton died very close to the time that, years before, he had predicted by calculating his own horoscope, and that several of his academic colleagues 'did not forbear to whisper among themselves, that rather than there should be a mistake in the calculation, he sent up his soul to heaven through a slip about his neck'.[9] But this anecdote was one that was repeated in connection with several astrologers of the age and is highly unlikely to have any basis in fact, especially given that Burton was buried in Christ Church Cathedral.

Like the title page of his book, Burton's memorial stone does not give his own name. Instead, it uses his literary pseudonym: 'Paucis notus, paucioribus ignotus, hic jacet Democritus Junior, cui vitam dedit et mortem Melancholia' ('Known to few, unknown to fewer, here lies Democritus Junior, to whom Melancholy gave life and death'). That melancholy gave him life through his occupation in years of reading and writing, and through the income generated by his book's sales, is clear. More enigmatic is the suggestion that melancholy brought him death, and perhaps this is the source of the rumour reported by Wood and Kennett.

It is characteristic of the man that his final words are both mysterious and mischievous, concealing his real identity behind the persona that made him famous. Wood reports that though many people thought Burton a 'severe student, a devourer of authors, a melancholy and humorous person' (that is, moody due to humoral imbalance), those who knew him well found him to be 'a person of great honesty, plain dealing and charity', while his colleagues at Christ Church said that 'his company was very merry, facete [witty] and juvenile'.[10] That intertwining of seriousness, exuberance, and elusiveness is shot through the *Anatomy* – the work that made him well known, but within the threads of which he chose to remain hidden.

Though the words on his tomb might imply that his cures for melancholy do not work, the paradox they inhabit suggests playfulness too. Burton is Democritus Junior to the last, a lifelong devotee of melancholy, or perhaps a slave to it. And for Burton, therapy for melancholy needs to be an enduring process, not a one-time cure. It requires painstaking application over many years to recover or at least to stave off the worst of it. André du Laurens says that daily experience teaches us 'that all melancholic diseases, are rebellious, long, and very hard to cure'; therefore, endless patience is needed.[11] Just as Burton could not leave off adding more and more to his book, so a sufferer should keep finding new ways to 'be not solitary, be not idle' (iii.431). Those six words with which Burton ends *The Anatomy of Melancholy* show that the directions for treating this protean condition need not be complex at all. To fulfil them, nonetheless, may take a lifetime's work.

Robert Burton, 'The Author's Abstract of Melancholy'[1]

When I go musing all alone,
Thinking of divers things fore-known,
When I build castles in the air,
Void of sorrow and void of fear,
Pleasing myself with phantasms sweet,
Methinks the time runs very fleet.
  All my joys to this are folly,
  Naught so sweet as melancholy.

When I lie waking all alone,
Recounting what I have ill done,
My thoughts on me then tyrannise,
Fear and sorrow me surprise,
Whether I tarry still or go,
Methinks the time moves very slow.
  All my griefs to this are jolly,
  Naught so mad as melancholy.

When to myself I act and smile,
With pleasing thoughts the time beguile,
By a brook side or wood so green,
Unheard, unsought for, or unseen,
A thousand pleasures do me bless,
And crown my soul with happiness.
  All my joys besides are folly,
  None so sweet as melancholy.

When I lie, sit, or walk alone,
I sigh, I grieve, making great moan,
In a dark grove, or irksome den,
With discontents and Furies then,
A thousand miseries at once
Mine heavy heart and soul ensconce,
  All my griefs to this are jolly,
  None so sour as melancholy.

Methinks I hear, methinks I see,
Sweet music, wondrous melody,
Towns, palaces, and cities fine;
Here now, then there; the world is mine,
Rare beauties, gallant ladies shine,
Whate'er is lovely or divine.
  All other joys to this are folly,
  None so sweet as melancholy.

Methinks I hear, methinks I see
Ghosts, goblins, fiends; my phantasy
Presents a thousand ugly shapes,
Headless bears, black men, and apes,
Doleful outcries, and fearful sights,
My sad and dismal soul affrights.
  All my griefs to this are jolly,
  None so damned as melancholy.

Methinks I court, methinks I kiss,
Methinks I now embrace my mistress.
O blessed days, O sweet content,
In Paradise my time is spent.
Such thoughts may still my fancy move,
So may I ever be in love.
  All my joys to this are folly,
  Naught so sweet as melancholy.

When I recount love's many frights,
My sighs and tears, my waking nights,
My jealous fits; O mine hard fate
I now repent, but 'tis too late.
No torment is so bad as love,
So bitter to my soul can prove.
    All my griefs to this are jolly,
    Naught so harsh as melancholy.

Friends and companions get you gone,
'Tis my desire to be alone;
Ne'er well but when my thoughts and I
Do domineer in privacy.
No gem, no treasure like to this,
'Tis my delight, my crown, my bliss.
  All my joys to this are folly,
  Naught so sweet as melancholy.

'Tis my sole plague to be alone,
I am a beast, a monster grown,
I will no light nor company,
I find it now my misery.
The scene is turned, my joys are gone;
Fear, discontent, and sorrows come.
  All my griefs to this are jolly,
  Naught so fierce as melancholy.

I'll not change life with any king,
I ravished am: can the world bring
More joy, than still to laugh and smile,
In pleasant toys time to beguile?
Do not, O do not trouble me,
So sweet content I feel and see.
  All my joys to this are folly,
  None so divine as melancholy.

I'll change my state with any wretch
Thou canst from jail or dunghill fetch;
My pain's past cure, another hell,
I may not in this torment dwell.
Now desperate I hate my life,
Lend me a halter or a knife;
  All my griefs to this are jolly,
  Naught so damned as melancholy.

CONCLUSION

The Two Faces of Melancholy

Before Robert Burton begins to anatomise the causes, symptoms, and cures of melancholy, he offers his reader a poem. Or is it a song? The refrain might make us want to sing along, and when Stan's Cafe adapted *The Anatomy of Melancholy* for the stage (Figure 10.1), they did exactly that – to the accompaniment of a lute. While the odd verses end with 'sweet' melancholy, elevated to 'divine' at the end, the even ones only decline: the closing line goes from 'mad' and 'sour' to 'damned' melancholy.

The poem-song captures two alternate states of being. On the one hand, to be melancholy is to indulge in a condition of pleasure and leisure: the mind drifts off on flights of fancy ('phantasms') while the body rests by a shady stream. On the other, it is to occupy, unwillingly, a place of anxiety, self-recrimination, and grief. With each stanza, these two conditions stretch further apart. The cheerful melancholic starts seeing things. The gloomy melancholic does too, but these are objects of terror, not delight: ghosts, goblins, demons. One falls in love and imagines his mistress before him, embracing him. The other is tormented by jealousy and suspicion. While one melancholic rejoices in the freedom of solitude, the other is tortured by it. As the scene ends, one is in a state of rapt delusion; the other is contemplating suicide.

But although the verses are like a debate, the two voices are by no means independent of one another. When John

FIGURE 10.1 Graeme Rose, Gerard Bell, Craig Stephens, and Rochi Rampal in *The Anatomy of Melancholy*, dir. James Yarker (Stan's Cafe, 2013).

Milton wrote his two companion poems 'L'Allegro' and 'Il Penseroso' – which may have been inspired by Burton's work – he created two distinct poetic personas: the cheerful speaker who rejects 'loathed Melancholy' and seeks out mirth, and the pensive speaker who embraces 'divinest Melancholy' and the wisdom of scholarship and meditation.[1] The two poems stand opposite one another, offering competing modes of living.

In Burton's version, by contrast, the voices intertwine. Are there two melancholics, speaking up for the respective joys and miseries which they each experience? Or is there only one, oscillating between delight and grief, becoming sicker and sicker as the speaker is pushed further towards mania and despair? Perhaps, for the modern reader, the poem captures something akin to the mood swings of bipolar disorder, where each stanza represents an interval of cheerfulness or despondency in the sufferer's state of mind.

For Burton's speaker, there is nothing noble or to be celebrated about the darkness of melancholy. Milton's 'Il Penseroso' reveres it:

But hail thou goddess, sage and holy,
Hail divinest Melancholy,
Whose saintly visage is too bright
To hit the sense of human sight. (lines 11–14)

Whereas this goddess Melancholy promises the grave wisdom of the cloister and the contemplative insight of the hermitage, Burton's only brings plague: it is the tyrant, the tormentor. His speaker is no Ficinian melancholic genius, and there is nothing desirable or fashionable about an experience that only seems to rob the sufferer of dignity: 'I'll change my state with any wretch / Thou canst from jail or dunghill fetch'.

But if this picture suggests only gloom, the poem-song is hardly sombre. After all, its rhyme words for 'melancholy' are 'jolly' and 'folly'. The melancholy we have encountered throughout this book is a condition of real suffering. At the same time, it is a subversive and disruptive force. There are kings who believe they are made of glass; peasants who believe they are kings; men whose laughing fits last for three days; women who purge rocks and live eels. Melancholy threatens to turn the world upside down, shatter the social order. It breaks the bounds of acceptable behaviour and makes even aristocrats become outsiders.

Curing melancholy is in part a conservative task, performed with the aims of moderating wayward passions and curbing excessive humours, while emphasising personal responsibility. But health can also be restored through outlandish performances where physicians become theatrical impresarios. A house is set on fire so that a man who cannot urinate relieves himself. A physician slips a snake into the vomit of a woman who is convinced she has swallowed one. A doctor's assistant dresses up as a corpse and sits in a coffin eating, to cure a patient who thinks he is dead and will take no sustenance.

And while a Galenic understanding of cure is that illness should be treated through restoring bodily proportion, Robert Burton does it through disproportionate means. Timothy Bright's *Treatise of Melancholy* (1586) is 80,000 words long. André du Laurens' 'Discourse of Melancholy' (from the longer work *A Discourse of the Preservation of the Sight*, 1599) is 30,000. By its sixth edition, *The Anatomy of Melancholy* (1651) stretches to over 500,000 words. It is a wildly excessive text, attempting to capture not only what a sufferer needs to know about the disease, but everything that has ever been said about it (and a good deal else). Burton hopes that his writings will work on readers as both recreation and cure, 'like gilded pills, which are so composed as well to tempt the appetite and deceive the palate, as to help and medicinally work upon the whole body' (iii.7). Yet the sheer size of it makes the work a large pill to swallow.

Nonetheless, the appetite for Burton's book was substantial in his own day. It saw eight editions over the course of the seventeenth century, and early copies show that his readers actively engaged with it: they underlined it, wrote in the margins, and sometimes disagreed with it. One reader was so disconcerted (or entertained) by

Burton's abrupt change of course from praising 'divine, rare, superexcellent tobacco' to condemning 'damned tobacco', that he or she wrote in the margin 'now you are mad'.[2] Several copied out Burton's lists of medicines or added them to recipes gleaned from other books, creating their own compilations of cures for melancholy.

Yet the *Anatomy*'s appeal has always gone beyond the merely functional. Readers have browsed it and pilfered from it: in the later seventeenth century, David Lloyd recommended it for gentlemen short of time, who, 'put to an aftergame of learning, pick many choice things to furnish them for discourse or writing'. For his novel *Tristram Shandy* (1758), Laurence Sterne borrowed whole passages without acknowledgement. Though Burton recommended that melancholics go to bed at regular times, his writing has kept readers awake: in 1650, John Gadsbury was reading the *Anatomy* in bed when a stray reference to horoscopes puzzled him so much that it prompted him to become an astrologer. It has also woken them up: that famous melancholic sufferer Samuel Johnson described the *Anatomy* as 'the only book that ever took him out of bed two hours sooner than he wished to rise', as if its curiosity forced him to read it against his will.[3]

Though it was not reprinted during the eighteenth century, it continued to be read and was a source of fascination for Romantic writers. Burton's account of how love could be generated through artifical means provided John Keats with the source for his *Lamia* (1820), the story of a shape-shifting, serpentine enchantress. When the book did once again reach the press, Charles Lamb objected:

> I do not know a more heartless sight than the reprint of the Anatomy of Melancholy. What need was there of unearthing the bones of that fantastic old great man, to expose them in a winding-sheet of the newest fashion to modern censure? What hapless stationer could dream of Burton ever becoming popular?[4]

The nineteenth and twentieth centuries saw a revival of interest in affordable copies, though the text is a challenge to the bookbinder's skills: the 1,400 pages of the New York Review Books paperback edition (2001) are held together by generous pastings of glue. It is a book of books – so much so that George Eliot quotes from it in *Middlemarch* to evoke Mr Casaubon, the man who spends his life fruitlessly attempting to write a similarly syncretic book, the 'Key to all Mythologies': 'Hard students are commonly troubled with gowts, catarrhs, rheums, cachexia, bradypepsia, bad eyes, stone, and collick, crudities, oppilations, vertigo, winds, comsumptions, and all such diseases as come by over-much sitting.'[5] In its most recent reinvention, Burton's book has shape-shifted into a play: Stan's Cafe's 2013 stage adaptation has four actors (mirroring the four humours, perhaps), performing a condensed version of the entire book with the aid of flipcharts, anatomical diagrams, and a potted hellebore plant. They take notes as they go, as if they are adding more and more content to this ever-expanding chronicle of melancholy. In their 2020 online lockdown version, the actors are 'penned up' like Democritus Junior in his study (i.17), and the gathered voices of Burton's text discuss melancholy through video-conferencing software, nearly four hundred years after the *Anatomy*'s first publication.[6]

Melancholy persists. Though the medical theories from which it sprang have long since been discredited, it retains a hold on our cultural imagination. Modern-day melancholia, inspired by the Ficinian notion of melancholic genius, has come to take on an aesthetic sense: as an artistic mood, an attitude of studied introspection, a palette of muted tones. But that is only a diluted form of the condition that afflicted Renaissance men and women and inspired Burton's writing: a tyrannising, feral condition with far rougher edges.

Because melancholy is about the capacity of humans to resist reason, its unruly force is also enlivening. It finds its centre in the many ways we are defined not merely by our capacity to think, but also by how we feel and imagine – ways that are not always tied to reality. And while melancholy hurts, it also gives signs of life. The antidotes to melancholy are life-giving too: if we remain curious, Burton suggests, we have not lost all hope.

Speaking of melancholy's persistence in individual bodies, Burton figures the disease as impossible to erase: 'as in Mercury's weather-beaten statue, that was once all over gilt, the open parts were clean, yet there was *in fimbriis aurum*, in the chinks a remnant of gold: there will be some relics of melancholy left in the purest bodies (if once tainted), not so easily to be rooted out' (i.430). But they are still gold.

ENDNOTES

Introduction

1. American Psychiatric Association, *Diagnostic and Statistical Manual of Mental Disorders*, 5th edn (Arlington, VA: American Psychiatric Association, 2013); David Adam, 'On the Spectrum', *Nature*, 496 (25 April 2013), 416–18; British Psychological Society, *Response to the American Psychiatric Association: DSM-5 Development* (Leicester: British Psychological Society, 2011), p. 3.
2. William Shakespeare, *Hamlet*, 1.2.85, in *William Shakespeare: The Complete Works*, ed. John Jowett, Willliam Montgomery, Gary Taylor, and Stanley Wells, 2nd edn (Oxford: Clarendon Press, 2005).
3. Angus Gowland, 'The Problem of Early Modern Melancholy', *Past & Present*, 191 (2006), 77–120.
4. Aristotle, *Problems*, ed. and trans. Robert Mayhew (Cambridge, MA: Harvard University Press, 2011), 30.1 (p. 277) (the work was attributed to Aristotle in antiquity, but may be pseudonymous); Lawrence Babb, *The Elizabethan Malady: A Study of Melancholia in English Literature from 1580 to 1642* (East Lansing: Michigan State College Press, 1951), chap. 8.
5. Anthony Wood, *Athenae Oxonienses* (London, 1691), p. 535.
6. Desiderius Erasmus, *Praise of Folly*, trans. Betty Radice, in *Collected Works of Erasmus*, 89 vols. (University of Toronto Press, 1974–), vol. XXVII, pp. 120–1. The words are quoted by Burton, *Anatomy*, i.52.

7. Biographical details are taken from J. B. Bamborough, 'Burton, Robert (1577–1640), writer', *Oxford Dictionary of National Biography*, www.oxforddnb.com (accessed 7 August 2020).
8. See Nicolas K. Kiessling, *The Library of Robert Burton* (Oxford Bibliographical Society, 1988).
9. *Oxford English Dictionary*, 'melancholia', *n.*, 2.b, www.oed.com/view/Entry/115994 (accessed 31 August 2020).
10. *Oxford English Dictionary*, 'psychology', *n.*, www.oed.com/view/Entry/153907 (accessed 31 August 2020).
11. Oliver Sacks, *The Man Who Mistook His Wife for a Hat* (London: Picador, 2011), p. x.

1 *Sorrow and Fear*

1. *Oxford English Dictionary*, 'melancholy', *n.*1, www.oed.com/view/Entry/116007 (accessed 3 June 2020).
2. Timothy Bright, *A Treatise of Melancholy* (London, 1586), p. 1.
3. Aristotle, *On Rhetoric: A Theory of Civic Discourse*, trans. George A. Kennedy (New York: Oxford University Press, 1991), 2.5.1 (p. 139).
4. Ibn Sina (Avicenna), *De anima*, 4.4, trans. Dag Nikolaus Hasse, 'Arabic Philosophy and Averroism', in James Hankins (ed.), *The Cambridge Companion to Renaissance Philosophy* (Cambridge University Press, 2007), pp. 113–33 (122); Thomas Aquinas, *Summa theologiae*, 61 vols. (London: Eyre & Spottiswoode, 1964–81), vol. xxi, pp. 70–1 (I^{a} IIae q. 44 a. 4).
5. Michel de Montaigne, *The Complete Essays*, trans. M. A. Screech (London: Penguin, 1991), II:12, pp. 671–2.
6. Thomas Wright, *The Passions of the Minde* (London, 1604), p. 8.

7. *Oxford English Dictionary*, 'imbonity', *n*., www.oed.com/view/Entry/91698 (accessed 2 June 2020).
8. William Shakespeare, *The Merchant of Venice*, ed. John Drakakis (London: Arden Shakespeare, 2010), 1.1.1.
9. William Shakespeare, *Hamlet*, 2.2.245, 256–8, in *William Shakespeare: The Complete Works*, ed. Jowett, Montgomery, Taylor, and Wells.
10. I use the Geneva Bible translation.
11. Bright, *Treatise of Melancholy*, p. 107.
12. Burton is paraphrasing Wright, *Passions of the Minde*.
13. See Hesiod, *Theogony*, 520–5.

2 *Body and Mind*

1. Giambattista da Monte, *Consultationum medicarum opus absolutissimum* (Basle, 1565), columns 547–9. The case is recorded in the *Anatomy*, ii.65, 111.
2. *Oxford English Dictionary*, 'psychosomatic', *adj*., www.oed.com/view/Entry/153938 (accessed 16 June 2020).
3. See further Erin Sullivan, *Beyond Melancholy: Sadness and Selfhood in Renaissance England* (Oxford University Press, 2016).
4. *The Complete Poems of John Donne*, ed. Robin Robbins (Harlow: Longman, 2010).
5. Prudencio de Sandoval, *The History of Charles the Vth, Emperor and King of Spain* (London, 1703), pp. 450–1.
6. Jean Fernel, *Universa medicina* (Frankfurt, 1577), i.135.
7. Montaigne, *Complete Essays*, II:17, p. 729. The Latin quotation is adapted from Martial, *Epigrams*, 2.36.5. See further M. A. Screech, *Montaigne and Melancholy: The Wisdom of the Essays* (London: Duckworth, 1983), chap. 3.
8. Montaigne, *Complete Essays*, II:8, p. 433.
9. Bright, *Treatise of Melancholy*, p. 1.

10. Aristotle, *Problems*, 30.1 (p. 277); see pp. 274–5.
11. *Oxford English Dictionary*, 'black man', *n.*, www.oed.com/view/Entry/19745 (accessed 16 June 2020).
12. Jean Bodin, *The Six Bookes of a Common-weale*, trans. Richard Knolles (1606), pp. 552–60. See further Mary Floyd-Wilson, *English Ethnicity and Race in Early Modern Drama* (Cambridge University Press, 2003), pp. 67–86.
13. Floyd-Wilson, *English Ethnicity*, pp. 93–4.

3 The Supernatural

1. Simon Goulart, *Admirable and Memorable Histories Containing the Wonders of our Time*, trans. Edward Grimeston (London, 1607), p. 3. My account is based on Goulart's, pp. 1–6, and on Cornelius Gemma, *De naturae divinis characterismis* (Antwerp, 1575), Book 2, pp. 201–16.
2. Barbara H. Traister, 'New Evidence about Burton's Melancholy?', *Renaissance Quarterly*, 29 (1976), 66–70; Lauren Kassell, Michael Hawkins, Robert Ralley, John Young, Joanne Edge, Janet Yvonne Martin-Portugues, and Natalie Kaoukji (eds.), 'Robert Burton (PERSON1483)', *The Casebooks of Simon Forman and Richard Napier, 1596–1634: A Digital Edition*, https://casebooks.lib.cam.ac.uk/identified-entities/PERSON1483 (accessed 21 August 2020).
3. See *Anatomy*, ed. Faulkner *et al.*, vol. IV, p. 235.
4. As Burton's Oxford editors note (*Anatomy*, ed. Faulkner *et al.*, vol. IV, p. 233) his source for the story of the Pied Piper of Hamelin is Johann Georg Gödelmann, *Tractatus de magis* (Frankfurt, 1601), though the traditional date that this happened was in 1284.
5. Reginald Scot, *The Discoverie of Witchcraft* (London, 1584), pp. 57–8.
6. Ibid., p. 57.

7. The story is told in Francesco Petrarca (Petrarch), *Epistolae familiares*, 1.3.
8. See Jeremy Schmidt, *Melancholy and the Care of the Soul: Religion, Moral Philosophy and Madness in Early Modern England* (Aldershot: Ashgate, 2007); Julius H. Rubin, *Religious Melancholy and Protestant Experience in America* (Oxford University Press, 1993).
9. See *Anatomy*, ed. Faulkner *et al.*, vol. VI, p. 256. Lives of Matthew Hamont and William Hacket can be found in the *Oxford Dictionary of National Biography*, www.odnb.com; Peter Burchett's story is mentioned in the biography of Sir John Hawkins.

4 *Delusions*

1. André du Laurens, *A Discourse of the Preservation of the Sight: Of Melancholike Diseases; of Rheumes, and of Old Age*, trans. Richard Surphlet (London, 1599), p. 103.
2. Robert Hooke gives a detailed description of his experiments with these glass drops in *Micrographia* (London, 1665), pp. 33–44.
3. *Oxford English Dictionary*, 'silly', *adj.*, 2, 4, 6, www.oed.com/view/Entry/179761 (accessed 18 June 2020); André du Laurens, *Discours de la conservation de la veue* (Rouen, 1615), fol. 105[v].
4. *Oxford English Dictionary*, 'conceit', n., 1.a, 8.a, www.oed.com/view/Entry/38074 (accessed 18 June 2020). For examples of Burton's usages, see the *Anatomy*, i.407.
5. Theodore Turquet de Mayerne, *Opera medica* (London, 1703), pp. 144–54; Isaac Casaubon, *Ephemerides*, ed. John Russell, 2 vols. (Oxford, 1850), vol. II, pp. 1242–9.
6. Du Laurens, *Discourse of the Preservation of Sight*, pp. 101–2; *Anatomy*, i.403.

7. Michael C. Schoenfeldt, *Bodies and Selves in Early Modern England: Physiology and Inwardness in Spenser, Shakespeare, Herbert, and Milton* (Cambridge University Press, 1999), p. 3.
8. Thomas Milles, *The Treasurie of Ancient and Modern Times* (London, 1613), pp. 154–5.
9. See Du Laurens, *Discourse of the Preservation of Sight*, pp. 102–3.
10. Burton describes al-Razi's three degrees of symptoms in the *Anatomy*, i.407; they are taken from al-Razi, *Almansor*, Book 9, an encyclopaedic survey of diseases in head-to-toe order which was available in a number of Latin versions, from Gerard of Cremona's translation in the twelfth century to Andreas Vesalius' paraphrase in the sixteenth.
11. Gill Speak, 'An Odd Kind of Melancholy: Reflections on the Glass Delusion in Europe (1440–1680)', *History of Psychiatry*, 1 (1990), 191–206 (esp. p. 193).
12. Du Laurens, *Discourse of the Preservation of Sight*, p. 102.
13. A modern-day case of a glass delusion was reported by Andy Lamejin in the Netherlands; *The Glass Delusion*, BBC Radio 4, first broadcast 8 May 2015, www.bbc.co.uk/programmes/b05sy63b; Victoria Shepherd, 'The People who Think they are Made of Glass', *BBC News Magazine*, 8 May 2015, www.bbc.co.uk/news/magazine-32625632 (both accessed 22 June 2020).
14. Miguel de Cervantes, *The Licenciate Vidriera; Or, Doctor Glass-Case, in The Exemplary Novels of Miguel de Cervantes Saavedra*, trans. Walter K. Kelly (London, 1855), p. 97.
15. Du Laurens, *Discourse of the Preservation of Sight*, p. 97.
16. [Thomas Tomkis], *Lingua* (London, 1607), sigs. B3^{v}–B4^{r}.
17. Du Laurens, *Discourse of the Preservation of Sight*, p. 98.
18. Laure Murat, *The Man Who Thought He Was Napoleon: Toward a Political History of Madness*, trans. Deke Dusinberre (University of Chicago Press, 2014), p. 107.

19. William Shakespeare, *The Taming of the Shrew*, ed. Barbara Hodgdon (London: Bloomsbury, 2014), Induction 2.128–9.
20. Swift's *A Tale of a Tub* (1704) is also indebted to *The Anatomy of Melancholy*. See further Angus Ross, '*The Anatomy of Melancholy* and Swift', John Irwin Fischer, Hermann J. Real, and James Woolley (eds.), *in Swift and his Contexts* (New York: AMS Press, 1989), 133–58; Christopher Tilmouth, 'Sceptical Perspectives on Melancholy: Burton, Swift, Pope, Sterne', *Review of English Studies*, 68 (2017), 924–44.
21. Jonathan Swift, *Gulliver's Travels* (London, 1826), p. 59.

5 *Love and Sex*

1. Josephus Struthius, *Ars sphygmica seu pulsum doctrina* (Basle, 1602), pp. 218–19.
2. See D. Evan Bedford, 'The Ancient Art of Feeling the Pulse', *British Heart Journal*, 13 (1951), 423–37.
3. *Sir Philip Sidney: The Major Works*, ed. Katherine Duncan-Jones (Oxford University Press, 1994), Sonnet 6, line 4; cf. Burton, *Anatomy*, iii.136.
4. Brian Levack, *The Devil Within: Possession and Exorcism in the Christian West* (New Haven, CT: Yale University Press, 2013), p. 172.
5. Jacques Ferrand, *Erotomania* (London, 1640), p. 11.
6. See further Julia Schiesari, *The Gendering of Melancholia: Feminism, Psychoanalysis, and the Symbolics of Loss in Renaissance Literature* (Ithaca, NY: Cornell University Press, 1992); Matthew Bell, *Melancholia: The Western Malady* (Cambridge University Press, 2014), pp. 76–97.
7. Margaret Cavendish wrote several poems on the subject, including 'A Dialogue between Melancholy and Mirth' and 'Of Melancholy'. On female humoral temperaments,

see Gail Kern Paster, 'The Unbearable Coldness of Female Being: Women's Imperfection and the Humoral Economy', *English Literary Renaissance*, 28 (1998), 416–40.

8. Ferrand, *Erotomania*, pp. 26, 66.
9. Hippocrates, *Epidemics*, 6.3.5, 14.
10. Ferrand, *Erotomania*, p. 107.
11. Ferrand, *Erotomania*, p. 121; Ovid, *Metamorphoses, Vol. 1: Books 1–8*, trans. Frank Justus Miller, rev. G. P. Goold (Cambridge, MA: Harvard University Press, 1989), 4. 266–7.
12. Ferrand, *Erotomania*, pp. 122–3.
13. Du Laurens, *Discourse of the Preservation of Sight*, p. 118.
14. William Shakespeare, *Romeo and Juliet*, ed. René Weis (London: Bloomsbury, 2012), 2.2.8–9. Burton quotes from the play when he discusses the sometimes fatal prognostics of love melancholy (iii.187).
15. Ferrand, *Erotomania*, pp. 117–18.
16. Ficino is commenting on Plato's *Symposium*, *Oratio* 7.10; see *Anatomy*, ed. Faulkner *et al.*, vol. VI, p. 65. On theories of vision, see Stuart Clark, *Vanities of the Eye: Vision in Early Modern European Culture* (Oxford University Press, 2007), esp. chap. 1.
17. Du Laurens, *Discourse of the Preservation of Sight*, p. 120.
18. William Shakespeare, *Much Ado About Nothing*, ed. Claire McEachern (London: Bloomsbury, 2007), 5.2.35–6, 39–40.
19. Du Laurens, *Discourse of the Preservation of Sight*, pp. 121–4.

6 Despair

1. Nathaniel Bacon, *A Relation of the Fearful Estate of Francis Spira* (Boston, 1762), p. 25.
2. See further Clare Costley King'oo, *Miserere Mei: The Penitential Psalms in Late Medieval and Early Modern England* (University of Notre Dame Press, 2012).
3. See Schmidt, *Melancholy and the Care of the Soul*, pp. 47–82.

4. See Michael MacDonald, 'The Fearefull Estate of Francis Spira: Narrative, Identity, and Emotion in Early Modern England', *Journal of British Studies*, 31 (1992), 32–61.
5. Bacon, *Fearful Estate of Francis Spira*, p. 8.
6. Ibid., p. 12.
7. Ibid., p. 13.
8. Ibid., pp. 14–15.
9. Ibid., p. 21.
10. Ibid., p. 36.
11. Ibid., p. 33.
12. See Matteo Gribaldi, *A Notable and Marvailous Epistle*, trans. Edward Aglionby (Worcester, 1550).
13. Bacon, *Fearful Estate of Francis Spira*, pp. 18, 32.
14. Christopher Marlowe, *Dr Faustus*, in *'Dr Faustus' and Other Plays*, ed. David Bevington and Eric Rasmussen (Oxford University Press, 1995), A-Text, 5.2.27–8.
15. John Bunyan, *'Grace Abounding' and Other Spiritual Autobiographies*, ed. John Stachniewski with Anita Pacheco (Oxford University Press, 1998), pp. 45, 93.
16. See Rhonda L. Blair, 'Robert Burton's "Agony": A Pattern of Revision Made for the Sixth Edition of *The Anatomy of Melancholy*', *Papers of the Bibliographical Society of America*, 78 (1984), 215–18.
17. *Oxford English Dictionary*, 'suicide', *n.*, www.oed.com/view/Entry/193691 (accessed 3 July 2020); cf. Shakespeare, *Hamlet*, 1.2.131–2.
18. Bright, *Treatise of Melancholy*, p. 184.

7 *The Non-Naturals*

1. *The Adages of Erasmus*, selected by William Barker (University of Toronto Press, 2001), p. 17; Erasmus quotes Cicero, *Letter to Atticus*, who alludes to the proverb by the single word 'prevention'. On the regimens, see Paul Slack,

'Mirrors of Health and Treasures of Poor Men: The Uses of the Vernacular Medical Literature of Tudor England', in Charles Webster (ed.), *Health, Medicine and Mortality in the Sixteenth Century* (Cambridge University Press, 1979), pp. 237–73.

2. Joannes de Mediolano (attrib.), *The Englishmans Docter, Or, The Schoole of Salerne*, trans. Sir John Harington (London, 1607), sig. A6r.
3. *Oxford English Dictionary*, 'incubus', *n.*, 2, www.oed.com/view/Entry/94101 (accessed 7 July 2020).
4. *Oxford English Dictionary*, 'cockney', *n.*, 2, www.oed.com/view/Entry/35467 (accessed 8 July 2020).
5. For a detailed study of hygiene practices and ideas of cleanliness in this period, see Susan North, *Sweet and Clean? Bodies and Clothes in Early Modern England* (Oxford University Press, 2020).
6. *Oxford English Dictionary*, 'parietines', *n.*, www.oed.com/view/Entry/137902 (accessed 8 July 2020).
7. Izaak Walton, *The Compleat Angler* (London, 1653), pp. 28–9. Burton's description of fishing is not altogether original, being largely based on *The Treatyse on Fysshing with an Angle* (1496); see *Anatomy*, ed. Faulkner *et al.*, vol. v, p. 165.
8. Laurens, *Discourse of the Preservation of the Sight*, p. 106.
9. See *Anatomy*, ed. Faulkner *et al.*, vol. II, p. 312.
10. Bright, *Treatise of Melancholy*, p. 243; *Anatomy*, i.300–30.

8 Medicine and Surgery

1. Bright, *Treatise of Melancholy*, pp. 265–6.
2. For a brief guide to medical practitioners in England, see the Early Modern Practitioners database, http://practitioners.exeter.ac.uk/practitioners (accessed 13 July 2020).

3. Pliny the Elder, *Natural History*, 25.21–5. A copy of the Fool's Cap World Map is held by the National Maritime Museum, Greenwich, London (G201:1/43); https://collections.rmg.co.uk/collections/objects/206385.html (accessed 4 August 2020).
4. On Carneades, see Pliny the Elder, *Natural History*, 25.21; *Anatomy*, ii.231.
5. I have corrected the misspelling of the man's name, 'Malatesta' in Holbrook Jackson's edition, to the form Burton uses; cf. *Anatomy*, ed. Faulkner *et al.*, vol. II, p. 234.
6. See *Anatomy*, ed. Faulkner *et al.*, vol. I, p. xvii; Eleanor Chance, Christina Colvin, Janet Cooper, C. J. Day, T. G. Hassall, Mary Jessup, and Nesta Selwyn, 'Markets and Fairs', in Alan Crossley and C. R. Elrington (eds.), *A History of the County of Oxford: Volume 4, the City of Oxford* (London, 1979), pp. 305–12, available at *British History Online*, www.british-history.ac.uk/vch/oxon/vol4/pp305-312 (accessed 16 July 2020).
7. Homer, *Odyssey: Books 1–12*, trans. A. T. Murray, rev. George E. Dimock (Cambridge, MA: Harvard University Press, 2019), 4.219–21.
8. *Anatomy*, ii.220, quoting Geoffrey Chaucer, *The Canterbury Tales*, General Prologue, 443–4.
9. William Shakespeare, *Hamlet*, ed. Ann Thompson and Neil Taylor (London: Thomson Learning, 2006), 5.2.248–51. Interestingly, in the second Quarto of *Hamlet* Claudius says that he will drop in an 'Onixe'. This is usually taken as a misreading for 'union' (ibid., 5.2.249n.) but onyx was known to be effective for preserving 'the vigour and good estate of the whole body' (*Anatomy*, ii.218). The story of Cleopatra dissolving a pearl is told by Pliny the Elder, *Natural History*, 9.58.

9 Lifting the Spirits

1. Despite the pseudonym, Burton's identity was widely known and the *Anatomy* was known as 'Burton's Melancholy' in the seventeenth century. In the first edition (1621), he ended the work with a conclusion which he used to unmask himself, signing it from his study in Christ Church, Oxford, with the name of Robert Burton. In all later editions, he removed this section and, with it, his own name. Nonetheless, scattered clues to his identity persist, as in references to his family; see *Anatomy*, ed. Faulkner *et al.*, vol. II, p. 66; vol. III, pp. 469–73.
2. *The Aphorisms of Hippocrates*, trans. Elias Marks from the Latin version of Verhoofd (New York: Collins, 1817), 1.1 (p. 29).
3. Rodericus à Fonseca, *Consultationes medicae* (Venice, 1620), p. 239, cited in *Anatomy*, ii.109; see *Anatomy*, ed. Faulkner *et al.*, vol. V, p. 193.
4. Du Laurens, *Discourse of the Preservation of Sight*, pp. 106–7; *Anatomy*, ii.114.
5. Du Laurens, *Discourse of the Preservation of Sight*, p. 107.
6. Bright, *Treatise of Melancholy*, pp. 247–8.
7. Ibid., p. 248; *Oxford English Dictionary*, 'Roaring Meg', *n.*, www.oed.com/view/Entry/166566 (accessed 23 July 2020).
8. White Kennett, *A Register and Chronicle Ecclesiastical and Civil* (London, 1728), p. 321.
9. Wood, *Athenae Oxonienses*, p. 535.
10. Ibid., p. 535.
11. Du Laurens, *Discourse of the Preservation of Sight*, p. 107.

Robert Burton, 'The Author's Abstract of Melancholy'

1. The text is my own modernised edition of the poem as found in Robert Burton, *The Anatomy of Melancholy* (Oxford, 1651), sig. §4^{r-v}. I have omitted the Greek subtitle, meaning 'in the form of a debate'.

Conclusion: The Two Faces of Melancholy

1. John Milton, 'L'Allegro', line 1, and 'Il Penseroso', line 12, in *Milton: The Complete Shorter Poems*, ed. John Carey, 2nd edn (Harlow: Pearson, 2007).
2. Quoted in Mary Ann Lund, *Melancholy, Medicine and Religion in Early Modern England: Reading 'The Anatomy of Melancholy'* (Cambridge University Press, 2010), p. 201.
3. Quoted ibid., pp. 197–202, where other historical readers' responses to the *Anatomy* are surveyed.
4. Charles Lamb, 'Detached Thoughts on Books and Reading', in *The Works of Charles Lamb* (London, 1852), p. 420.
5. George Eliot, *Middlemarch*, ed. David Carroll (Oxford University Press, 1999), p. 39; cf. Burton, *Anatomy*, i.302.
6. The 35 episodes of Stan's Cafe's play *The Anatomy of Melancholy* are available via www.stanscafe.co.uk/project stans-internet-cafe.html (accessed 30 August 2020).

FURTHER READING

Editions of The Anatomy of Melancholy

There are two paperback editions:

1 ed. Holbrook Jackson, with an introduction by William H. Gass (New York Review Books, 2001)
2 ed. Angus Gowland (London: Penguin, 2020)

The standard scholarly edition is in six volumes (three of text, three of commentary) ed. Thomas C. Faulkner, Nicolas K. Kiessling, and Rhonda L. Blair; commentary by J. B. Bamborough with Martin Dodsworth (Oxford: Clarendon Press, 1989–2000).

Though there are several selected editions of the *Anatomy*, it is far more enjoyable to dip into the complete text and make your own selection – and Burton's structural method positively encourages it. For those who would prefer something slimmer than the 1,400 pages of the full work, an engaging alternative (and only 100 pages long) is *The Anatomy of Melancholy: Adapted for the Stage by Stan's Cafe* (Birmingham: Stan's Cafe, 2013).

Secondary Reading

Bell, Matthew, *Melancholia: The Western Malady* (Cambridge University Press, 2014)
Broomhall, Susan (ed.), *Early Modern Emotions: An Introduction* (London: Routledge, 2017)
Gowland, Angus, *The Worlds of Renaissance Melancholy: Robert Burton in Context* (Cambridge University Press, 2006)

Jackson, Stanley W., *Melancholia and Depression: From Hippocratic Times to Modern Times* (New Haven, CT: Yale University Press, 1986)

Klibansky, Raymond, Erwin Panofsky, and Fritz Saxl, *Saturn and Melancholy: Studies in the History of Natural Philosophy, Religion and Art* (London: Nelson, 1964)

Levack, Brian, *The Devil Within: Possession and Exorcism in the Christian West* (New Haven, CT: Yale University Press, 2013)

Lund, Mary Ann, *Melancholy, Medicine and Religion in Early Modern England: Reading 'The Anatomy of Melancholy'* (Cambridge University Press, 2010)

MacDonald, Michael, *Mystical Bedlam: Madness, Anxiety, and Healing in Seventeenth-Century England* (Cambridge University Press, 1981)

MacDonald, Michael, and Terence R. Murphy, *Sleepless Souls: Suicide in Early Modern England* (Oxford University Press, 1990)

McMahon, Darrin, *The Pursuit of Happiness: A History from the Greeks to the Present* (London: Allen Lane, 2006)

Radden, Jennifer, *Melancholic Habits: Burton's 'Anatomy' and the Mind Sciences* (Oxford University Press, 2017)

Moody Minds Distempered: Essays on Melancholy and Depression (Oxford University Press, 2009)

Schiesari, Julia, *The Gendering of Melancholia: Feminism, Psychoanalysis, and the Symbolics of Loss in Renaissance Literature* (Ithaca, NY: Cornell University Press, 1992)

Schmidt, Jeremy, *Melancholy and the Care of the Soul: Religion, Moral Philosophy and Madness in Early Modern England* (Aldershot: Ashgate, 2007)

Shirilan, Stephanie, *Robert Burton and the Transformative Powers of Melancholy* (Farnham: Ashgate, 2015)

Siraisi, Nancy G., *The Clock and the Mirror: Girolamo Cardano and Renaissance Medicine* (Princeton University Press, 1997)

Medieval and Early Renaissance Medicine: An Introduction to Knowledge and Practice (University of Chicago Press, 1990)

Stachniewski, John, *The Persecutory Imagination: English Puritanism and the Literature of Religious Despair* (Oxford: Clarendon Press, 1991)

Sullivan, Erin, *Beyond Melancholy: Sadness and Selfhood in Renaissance England* (Oxford University Press, 2016)

Trevor, Douglas, *The Poetics of Melancholy in Early Modern England* (Cambridge University Press, 2004)

Wear, Andrew, *Knowledge and Practice in English Medicine, 1550–1680* (Oxford University Press, 2000)

Wells, Susan, *Robert Burton's Rhetoric: An Anatomy of Early Modern Knowledge* (University Park: Pennsylvania State University Press, 2019)

Online Resources

A History of Delusions, 13 episodes, BBC Radio 4, first broadcast 30 November – 14 December 2018, https://www.bbc.co.uk/programmes/m0007rvd

Bright, Timothy, *A Treatise of Melancholie* (1586), e-book at HathiTrust Digital Library, https://hdl.handle.net/2027/mdp.49015000413873

Project Gutenberg, online full text of *The Anatomy of Melancholy* (2004), www.gutenberg.org/ebooks/10800

Stan's Cafe, online lockdown adaptation (2020) of their stage play *The Anatomy of Melancholy* in 35 short films; available via www.stanscafe.co.uk/project-stans-internet-cafe.html

'The Anatomy of Melancholy', *In Our Time*, BBC Radio 4, first broadcast 12 May 2011, www.bbc.co.uk/programmes/b010y30m

The New Anatomy of Melancholy, 10 episodes, BBC Radio 4, first broadcast 11–22 May 2020, www.bbc.co.uk/programmes/m000j1jq

INDEX